150
ENCOURAGING
BIBLE STUDIES
for Women

Grow
to Love
GOD'S
WORD

BARBOUR
PUBLISHING

READY TO FALL IN LOVE WITH GOD'S WORD?

Do you find it hard to make time for Bible study? You intend to do it, but the hours turn into days, and before you know it, another week has passed and you have not picked up God's Word. This book provides an avenue for you to open the Bible regularly and dig into a passage—even if you only have five minutes!

Minutes 1–2: ***Read*** carefully the scripture passage for each day's Bible study.

Minute 3: ***Understand.*** Ponder a couple of prompts designed to help you apply the verses from the Bible to your own life. Consider these throughout your day as well.

Minute 4: ***Apply.*** Read a brief devotional based on the day's scripture. Think about what you are learning and how to apply the scriptural truths to your own life.

Minute 5: ***Pray.*** A prayer starter will help you to begin a time of conversation with God. Remember to allow time for Him to speak into your life as well.

This beautiful book can help you to establish the discipline of studying scripture. Pour yourself a cup of coffee and make that first five minutes of your day count, or use these studies to end your day strong. You will find that spending even five minutes focused on scripture and prayer has the power to make a huge difference. Soon you will want to make time for even more time in God's Word!

GOD IS ALWAYS THE SAME

Read Psalm 102; Malachi 3:6; Hebrews 13:8; James 1:17

Key Verses:

You made the earth in the beginning. You made the heavens with Your hands. They will be destroyed but You will always live. They will all become old as clothing becomes old. You will change them like a coat. And they will be changed, but You are always the same. Your years will never end.
Psalm 102:25–27 nlv

Understand:

* What are the ways you enjoy change, and what are the things you wish would always stay the same?

* What changes cause you the most stress?

* In addition to Psalm 102, how do the scriptures in Malachi 3:6, Hebrews 13:8, and James 1:17 give you peace, knowing that God is unchanging?

Apply:

Life is always changing. Some of us thrive on that and some of us don't. We all have some things we love to change and other things we wish would always stay the same. No matter what changes we experience in our circumstances, relationships, and the world around us, it's so good to know that God is our one true constant. He is steady and strong and eternally true, and we can put all our faith in Him. We can build our lives on Him. We can trust that He is the perfect Creator with perfect plans and that He is sovereign over all places and times forever. That truth should fill us with a steady, strong peace that prevails throughout our lives.

Pray:

Heavenly Father, thank You for being the same yesterday, today, and forever. I need Your steady, unchanging presence and love every moment of my life. I need to remember that You always have been and always will be, and Your perfect plans for all of creation will prevail no matter what. Amen.

FAITHFUL FRIENDSHIP

Read RUTH 1

Key Verses:

> *Ruth replied, "Don't ask me to leave you and turn back. Wherever you go, I will go; wherever you live, I will live. Your people will be my people, and your God will be my God. Wherever you die, I will die, and there I will be buried. May the LORD punish me severely if I allow anything but death to separate us!"*
> RUTH 1:16–17 NLT

Understand:

* Orpah was conflicted at first, but then she decided to leave Naomi. What motivated Ruth's fierce loyalty to Naomi instead of choosing to go with Orpah?

* Have you ever felt as low as Naomi as described in Ruth 1:20–21? How did God lift you up?

Apply:

Every woman needs such a loyal woman in her life as Ruth was to Naomi. If you have that kind of faithful friend or relative, praise God for her and make sure she knows how grateful you are for her. Nurture that relationship. If you have more than one woman in your life like that, you are extremely blessed! And if you need a faithful friend, pray for God to help you make the connection. He knows and cares that you need good friendship, and He will help you find it. His Word says, "Two people are better off than one, for they can help each other succeed. If one person falls, the other can reach out and help. But someone who falls alone is in real trouble. Likewise, two people lying close together can keep each other warm. But how can one be warm alone? A person standing alone can be attacked and defeated, but two can stand back-to-back and conquer. Three are even better, for a triple-braided cord is not easily broken" (Ecclesiastes 4:9–12 NLT).

Pray:

Heavenly Father, thank You for the gift of loyal friendship. Please bless my friends, and help us grow in our relationships with each other and with You! Amen.

A CREATIVE CREATOR

Read GENESIS 1

Key Verse:

> *God saw all that he had made, and it was very good. And there was evening, and there was morning—the sixth day.*
> GENESIS 1:31 NIV

Understand:

* Consider the intricate details seen in nature. The petals of a flower that are arranged in a set pattern. The perfect curve of a nautilus shell. The instincts of a lion. Think of three examples of your own.

* If the world came about after a "big bang," as some scientists say, how could the detail seen in nature be explained?

Apply:

The book of Genesis begins with the words "In the beginning God created. . ." If God was already creating *in the beginning*, then that means He was not Himself created, but rather, He is the great Creator of all things.

God separated day from night. He made the stars, moon, and sun. He created the many varieties of trees and flowers, each one intricate in its design! God made all of the animals—the unique hippo and giraffe, the enormous elephant and whale, the majestic lion. . . . God is a creative Creator!

God's greatest creations were made in His image. Men, women, and children are special to God. We bear some of His traits. We are His masterpieces.

Remember to notice the details of God's glorious creation as you go about your day. Take care of the earth. It was designed by your Father. Respect all other people. They, like you, bear the image of God.

Pray:

Heavenly Father, You have made all things. You are the Creator who sustains life. You knit me together in my mother's womb. May I treat with great respect all of Your creation, even that which others may devalue. In Jesus' name I pray. Amen.

HOPE IN THE PIT

Read GENESIS 37

Key Verses:

> They said to one another, "Here comes this dreamer.
> Come now, let us kill him and throw him into one of the
> pits. Then we will say that a fierce animal has devoured
> him, and we will see what will become of his dreams."
>
> GENESIS 37:19–20 ESV

Understand:

* Joseph was thrown into the pit by his own brothers.
  Have you ever been betrayed by someone you trusted?
  How did you overcome?

* Even in the pit, Joseph never gave up. Maybe you've
  walked a mile in Joseph's shoes. How do you keep
  your head up, even when circumstances seem to be
  against you?

Apply:

Some would argue that young Joseph had it coming. All that
bragging about being the favored child didn't exactly put him
in good standing with his brothers, after all. Those dreams of

his were a source of contention among the siblings.

But imagine finding yourself at the bottom of a pit, bruised, dirty, and hurting, while those you thought you could trust jeered at you from above. The feelings of betrayal must have been overwhelming. Perhaps Joseph even wondered if those dreams of his had been from God or were the result of something bad he'd eaten.

Maybe you've been there. You've faced betrayal from someone you trusted—a husband, a parent, a child, a sibling, a friend. You're staring up, up, up from the bottom of a pit, your heart broken into a thousand pieces as your dreams seemingly come to an end.

Just remember, Joseph's story didn't end in the pit. God redeemed the situation and turned everything around. He'll do the very same for you. So don't give up. The Lord has big plans for you, and they're just around the corner.

Pray:

Father, I feel so betrayed. Those who claimed to care
about me turned their backs on me when I least suspected.
Like Joseph, I feel as if I'm in a pit. Rescue me, I pray.
Give me hope, comfort, and deliverance. Amen.

THE BURNING BUSH

Read EXODUS 3:1–17

Key Verse:

*"Do not come any closer," God said. "Take off your sandals,
for the place where you are standing is holy ground."*

EXODUS 3:5 NIV

Understand:

* Think of a time when you truly felt like you were in
  God's presence. What did it feel like?

* Picture yourself in Moses' sandals. What might he
  have thought as the Lord spoke to him through the
  burning bush?

Apply:

When you're walking through a stressful season and you're
looking for the perfect place to calm your nerves, the very
safest (and most peaceful) place is the presence of God.
When you cross over the invisible line into the holy of
holies, everything else disappears. Worries cease. Cares flee.
Troubles vanish. All the things that have kept your stomach
in knots have to go in His presence.

What's troubling you today? Can you, like Moses, stand in front of the burning bush and let go of the things that have held you in their grasp? Can you toss them into His fiery presence and see them consumed? God longs for you to live in peace, and your first step toward finding peace is getting into God's presence.

What's holding you back? Take off those sandals and run into His holy presence today.

Pray:

Lord, today I choose to spend quality time with You. I let go of my fears, my troubles, my anxieties. I place my hand in Yours and cross—feet bare—into Your holy presence. Thank You for what You're doing in my life, Lord. Amen.

THE WATER'S EDGE

Read PSALM 23

Key Verses:

> He makes me lie down in green pastures, he leads me
> beside quiet waters, he refreshes my soul. He guides
> me along the right paths for his name's sake.
> PSALM 23:2–3 NIV

Understand:

* Have you ever walked through a season where the
  Lord specifically instructed you to rest, to lie in green
  pastures beside still waters?

* What's the hardest thing about resting for you?

Apply:

He leads me beside still waters. How many times have you
quoted those words? But have you ever paused to consider
their meaning? When God leads us beside still waters, He's
drawing us away from the cares and anxieties of life, far from
the busyness, the harried schedule, the pressures of the day.
At the water's edge, things are calm, still. The only things
moving are the wind whispering through the trees and the

14

gentle waters of the brook below.

> *He leads me beside still waters. . .so that I can*
> *rest my mind, stop my crazy thoughts from*
> *tumbling through my brain, quiet my heart.*

> *He leads me beside still waters. . .so that my soul can*
> *be restored, my joy replenished, my hope resurrected.*

> *He leads me beside still waters so*
> *that anxieties will cease.*

Today, allow the Lord to take you by the hand and lead you beside still waters. You'll find all you need and more.

Pray:

> *Father, thank You for drawing me away from the chaos*
> *and the pain to a peaceful place with You. I willingly follow*
> *You to the still waters, that I might find peace. Amen.*

CALL UPON THE LORD

Read PSALMS 86:1–87:7

Key Verses:

> Give ear, O LORD, to my prayer; and attend to the
> voice of my supplications. In the day of my trouble
> I will call upon You, for You will answer me.
> PSALM 86:6–7 NKJV

Understand:

* When you run into trouble, whom do you call upon first? A friend? A family member?

* The psalmist states that he will call upon the Lord in his day of trouble. Why? What will the result most certainly be according to today's key verses?

Apply:

You know the type of day. Everything goes wrong. Just when you thought you were breaking even financially, your hot-water heater goes out. Or your property taxes go up drastically. Or the school is asking for more money for extracurricular activities. On top of that, no one in the family can seem to get along. Everyone is bickering. There is eye rolling, and the blame game is nonstop. Tattling and arguing are also abundant. You want to yell out, as the lady in the bubble bath commercial, "Calgon, take me away!"

When you have one of "those" days, whom do you tend to call first? Many women tend to pick up the phone to call a girlfriend, mom, or sister. Next time you are struggling, instead of heading for your cell phone, call on your heavenly Father. God is always there, and He cares. He wants you to turn to Him. He will answer.

Pray:

Lord, rather than dumping my troubles on my husband or mom, I will choose to call upon Your mighty name. My girlfriends and sisters can only do so much, but You are the sovereign God of the universe. You are big enough to handle even my very worst day. Thank You for hearing my prayers and answering when I am in trouble. Amen.

DAILY PURITY

Read 1 John 1:5–10

Key Verse:

> *If we confess our sins, he is faithful and just and will forgive us our sins and purify us from all unrighteousness.*
>
> 1 John 1:9 niv

Understand:

* Why is it important that God offers us forgiveness time and time again?

* Are you ever tempted to deny that you've sinned at all? What is the result?

* How does forgiveness feel on a heart level?

Apply:

We Christians talk a lot about forgiveness, and rightfully so. God's forgiveness and grace are essential to our faith and salvation. But God's forgiveness is a bigger concept than simply pardoning our sin. The forgiveness available to us through the blood of Jesus Christ purifies us just as if we had never sinned in the first place, leaving us holy, righteous, and blameless in the sight of God.

God's perfect forgiveness offers us purity. It makes us without blemish and whole. Because of that, we can stand confident before the King of kings and Lord of lords. These are the things we stand to gain when we humble ourselves and confess our sins to God. Confession leads to transformation as we grow to be more like Christ. There's no other way to start again, to join Him in the light of His goodness.

Start today in confession. Admit where you've failed. God is listening, and He will purify you again.

Pray:

Father, I come before You this morning seeking Your forgiveness. I messed up. . .again. My sin creates a divide between You and me, and I can't bear it. Although I feel unworthy to ask You to do it again, please purify my heart. Cover me in Your grace and make me righteous before You. Amen.

I FEEL BETRAYED

Read PSALM 41:9–13

Key Verse:

> *Even my close friend, someone I trusted, one who*
> *shared my bread, has turned against me.*
>
> PSALM 41:9 NIV

Understand:

* Verse 12 (NIV) of this passage says, "Because of my integrity you uphold me." How might you demonstrate integrity in your own situation?

* When hurt and bitterness overcome you, can you make a conscious effort to turn to God?

Apply:

There are few things that hurt more in life than being betrayed by someone we love, whether it's a friend, family member, or husband. Of course, all of us let each other down now and then; we're human and fallible. But betrayal goes deeper. It's a denial of the relationship we thought was so secure. It's like taking a step on what we took for granted was solid ground, only to find ourselves falling into a chasm. It may make us doubt ourselves and our own worth. The emotional anguish may make us sink into depression.

When the psalmist experienced this, he took his pain to God. Instead of begging his betrayer to change back into the person he thought he could count on, he asked God to be the one to restore his sense of balance and security. He affirmed God's love for him and praised God.

Pray:

> *Lord, help me to have integrity even in the midst of this pain. Thank You that Your love will never fail me. You will never betray me. I praise You! Amen.*

PERFECT HARMONY

Read COLOSSIANS 3:1–17

Key Verses:

> *Put on then, as God's chosen ones, holy and beloved, compassionate hearts, kindness, humility, meekness, and patience, bearing with one another and, if one has a complaint against another, forgiving each other; as the Lord has forgiven you, so you also must forgive. And above all these put on love, which binds everything together in perfect harmony. And let the peace of Christ rule in your hearts.*
>
> COLOSSIANS 3:12–15 ESV

Understand:

* Does the Word of Christ dwell in you richly?

* What is an example of setting your mind on things above instead of things of earth?

* What does it mean to do everything in the name of Jesus?

Apply:

Our days can be full of conflicts—little ones and big ones, with family members or friends, coworkers or managers, strangers at the store or in traffic. On a really bad day, maybe you've had conflict with all of them. Sometimes we handle conflicts well, and sometimes we don't. As you reflect on your day, you might smile with satisfaction over how you controlled your tongue in one setting but cringe at how you overreacted in another. Or you might still be holding on to lots of anger and frustration. Whatever the case, give it to God, and remember that His grace covers you. Ask Him to reveal your sin and show you where you need to forgive and to seek forgiveness. Let Him help you communicate well. Don't run from all conflict or difficult conversations tomorrow, but as you face them, remember that you are one of God's chosen. You can demonstrate a compassionate heart, kindness, meekness, and patience. You can give grace and forgiveness to others because you know how much grace and forgiveness God gives to you. Let His love bind everything together, and let His peace rule in your heart.

Pray:

Heavenly Father, please focus my mind on heavenly things, not the things of earth. Help me to rid my life of sin and fill it up with all the good things of You. I am one of Your chosen. I want to represent Your love and peace to others in everything I do. Amen.

ALL THINGS

Read ROMANS 8:18–30

Key Verse:

> *We know that God makes all things work together*
> *for the good of those who love Him and are*
> *chosen to be a part of His plan.*
> ROMANS 8:28 NLV

Understand:

* How does Romans 8:28 give you hope?

* Do you trust that God has good in store for you? Why or why not?

* What are you hopefully waiting for that you do not have now (see Romans 8:24)?

Apply:

Romans 8:28 ranks high on the list of verses that Christians commit to memory. You may have learned it as a song when you were a child or written it on an index card to remember the hope it carries: no matter what, God makes *all things* work together for the good of His children.

Not some things. Not just the easy things. Not just the

good things. All things. The hard things. The heartbreaking things. The frustrating things. The moments when it seems like nothing good can come, God is working it for our good.

The unspoken part of Romans 8:28 is that we're often waiting while He is working. And waiting is hard. But waiting with the promise of this verse brings hope. What are you hoping for today? Ask God to reveal His work to you as you wait. He is faithful to deliver on His promises in His time.

Pray:

Good, good Father, thank You for the hope of Your promise
that You're working all things together for my good. When I
don't understand what You are doing, it's hard for me to wait,
but still I hope. And I know my hope in You is never in vain.
Give me patience to wait on Your timing and Your plan. Amen.

YOU CAN CHOOSE JOY

Read PSALM 118

Key Verse:

> This is the day the LORD has made.
> We will rejoice and be glad in it.
> PSALM 118:24 NLT

Understand:

* What are some of the difficulties written about in Psalm 118?

* Why do you think the psalmist still chooses to praise God?

* How can you rejoice in today even if you are going through a hard season?

Apply:

Psalm 118 starts and ends in the same way: "Give thanks to the LORD, for he is good! His faithful love endures forever" (verses 1, 29 NLT). This statement of praise and appreciation for God bookends a chapter filled with great challenges and great victories. Through hostility and attacks from enemies, the psalm writer continues to come back to the fact that God is the rescuer, that He hears and answers prayer, that He puts purpose and joy in each day.

What if you started and ended your day in joyful appreciation for what God is doing? "Thank You, Lord, for being so good to me. Your faithful love endures forever!" This morning, set the stage for rejoicing in today, and tonight, before you lay your head on the pillow, thank Him again. Rejoice and be glad in today, knowing that God is working all things together for your good (see Romans 8:28)!

Pray:

God, today I am choosing joy. Not because everything is perfect and not because I feel overly happy. I'm choosing to rejoice in today because it is the day You made. And I know it is good because You are good. Thank You for loving me today and every day. Thank You for giving me a reason to rejoice! Amen.

FREE IN CHRIST

Read JOHN 8

Key Verses:

> Jesus replied, "Very truly I tell you, everyone who
> sins is a slave to sin. Now a slave has no permanent
> place in the family, but a son belongs to it forever.
> So if the Son sets you free, you will be free indeed."
>
> JOHN 8:34–36 NIV

Understand:

* How is a sinner freed from sin?

* What does it look like for you as a believer to be "free
  indeed" in today's society?

Apply:

Jesus' death on the cross paid the wages of our sin. He set us
free when we placed our trust in Him to do so. There is no
other way by which anyone can be saved except through Him.

We are set free from the sins of our past, and we are set
free from sin that easily entangles us. Living in a society that
is filled with temptation to sin is not easy, but as a believer,
you have the power to overcome temptation through Christ.

Thank your heavenly Father that you are no longer a slave to sin. Because of Jesus' death for you, you are completely free. You will never again be shackled by a lifestyle of sin, but instead, you will turn in repentance when you begin to take your eyes off Him and He will lead you back to His side. You are saved from sin, and yes, you are free indeed.

Pray:

> *Thank You, Jesus, for saving me from my sin.*
> *Thank You that because of my faith in You*
> *as Savior, I can be free indeed! Amen.*

A HARVEST OF RIGHTEOUSNESS AND PEACE

Read HEBREWS 12

Key Verse:

No discipline seems pleasant at the time, but painful. Later on, however, it produces a harvest of righteousness and peace for those who have been trained by it.
HEBREWS 12:11 NIV

Understand:

* How has discipline produced a good harvest in your life?

* What does it mean that "God is a consuming fire" (Hebrews 12:29 NIV)?

Apply:

The word *discipline* doesn't always bring peaceful thoughts to mind. We might think of angry arguments and punishments of the growing-up years and other kinds of consequences during rebellious times in our lives. But Hebrews 12 shows us how we *can* view discipline with peace—by realizing the hardship we endure is the discipline from God that is good for us in a loving, fatherly way. If we let Him,

He strengthens us and proves our faith this way—just like good parents shouldn't always rescue their children from every hard thing. Rather, they let them experience difficulty and consequences so that they can develop strength and confidence in their own capabilities, plus learn from their mistakes. Once we have grown up, we appreciate the discipline good parents gave us as we develop into mature adults who contribute well to the world around us. Likewise, once we have reached the other side of a particular hardship, we can see how God used it in our lives to develop us, plus to produce "a harvest of righteousness and peace" that contributes to His kingdom.

Pray:

*Heavenly Father, please help me to focus on hardship in
a positive way as good discipline from You. Teach me,
strengthen me, and develop me in the midst of it, and give
me peace that You are working it all for good. Amen.*

GOD HEARS YOU

Read 1 JOHN 5:13–20

Key Verses:

> *This is the confidence we have in approaching God:*
> *that if we ask anything according to his will, he hears*
> *us. And if we know that he hears us—whatever we*
> *ask—we know that we have what we asked of him.*
>
> 1 JOHN 5:14–15 NIV

Understand:

* Are you confident that God hears your prayers? Why or why not?

* How can you know your prayers are in line with God's will?

Apply:

From an early age, children are taught that praying is thanking God and asking Him for things that they need or want to happen. If we're not careful, we can incorrectly think of God as a heavenly vending machine that will dole out the goods if we say the right words and push the right buttons.

But prayer is *not* about pushing our agenda and hoping

God will be on board with it. Prayer is approaching our loving Father with a heart that sincerely wants to be in line with His. When we pray this way, the things we ask of Him will fit into His good and perfect will for our lives and His creation as a whole. And *that's* when He hears us and we will receive what we have asked for.

What is God's will? Ask Him to show you. Seek Him in His Word. Talk to friends who are strong in their faith, and see what God is doing in their lives. He's listening. He hears you.

Pray:

Father, I am confident in my prayers to You. Give me Your wisdom to approach You with requests that You will hear and grant. I long to be in the center of Your good and perfect plan, God. Amen.

THE SHELTER OF THE MOST HIGH

Read PSALM 91

Key Verse:

Whoever dwells in the shelter of the Most High
will rest in the shadow of the Almighty.
PSALM 91:1 NIV

Understand:

* Have you walked through a season where you needed God's protection and shelter? How did He take care of you?

* Have you ever had to shelter others under your wings?

Apply:

If you've ever had to run for cover during a rainstorm, you know that anything will do—an awning, a car, a shopping center, even a tent. Whatever serves to hold back the rain works just fine for you.

Shelters don't just keep out the rain; they provide a psychological covering as well. When you've got something over your head, you feel safer. That's how God wants you to feel when you run to Him with your troubles. When you hide under the shadow of His wings (as a baby chick would hide under its mother's wings), He's got you covered. He's like a papa bear, daring anyone to mess with His cub.

Here's an encouraging fact: God wants to keep you covered at all times. But let's face it. . .we have a way of tucking ourselves under other, counterfeit shelters. Maybe it's time to do an assessment, to make sure you've got the right covering. Whatever you're facing, God wants to protect you as you go through it.

Pray:

Thank You for the reminder that You're my protector, Lord! I'll do my best not to run to the counterfeit shelters when I've got the real deal. Amen.

HAVE YOU BEEN WITH JESUS?

Read ACTS 4

Key Verse:

> *Now when they saw the boldness of Peter and John,*
> *and perceived that they were uneducated and*
> *untrained men, they marveled. And they*
> *realized that they had been with Jesus.*
> ACTS 4:13 NKJV

Understand:

* Do others know that you have been with Jesus?
* How do they know, or why are they unsure?

Apply:

Peter and John had been with Jesus. It was evident. They were warned not to speak of Him, but they said this was not possible. They knew Jesus, and they could not be quieted.

These were blue-collar fishermen called as disciples of Christ. And yet they boldly preached and healed in the name of Christ.

When people examine your life, do they know you are a Christian? Do you stand out as a Christ follower? Do you find ways to bring Jesus into everyday conversations? Or are you more like the teenager who wants her dad to drop her off a block from school so that no one will know she is associated with him?

Consider these things. Dwell upon them. Pray about them. Make changes as needed. You want to be a woman who is known for having "been with Jesus."

Pray:

Lord Jesus, I will live boldly for You. I want to be known as one who walks with You. Examine my heart, Jesus. Point out to me areas where change needs to occur. I am not ashamed of You. I want to be bold like Peter and John. I want to be known as a Christian even if it is not popular in some circles. Amen.

SIMPLIFY

Read MATTHEW 25:31–46

Key Verse:

> "The King will reply, 'Truly I tell you, whatever
> you did for one of the least of these brothers
> and sisters of mine, you did for me.'"
> MATTHEW 25:40 NIV

Understand:

* What areas of life or relationships cause you the most
  concern about whether you are doing a good job or
  doing enough?

* How has your relationship with Jesus grown as you care
  for others in need?

Apply:

As women, we so often worry about whether or not we are
doing enough, doing the right things, and doing them well—
in our marriages, our parenting, our friendships, our homes,
our jobs, our ministry, and so on. Sometimes we need to
simplify and stop trying so hard. We need to ask God to help
us focus on the good things He planned for us to do when He

created us. We should ask Him to show us the relationships He wants us to invest in the most, starting with Him. And this scripture in Matthew should remind us that the very best job anyone can have is to serve our King by serving others. We are always doing the right thing if we are doing even the simplest act of kindness for someone in need. There is such peace and contentment when we realize how rewarding it is to care for others as if caring for Jesus Himself—because truly we are.

Pray:

Loving Savior, please remind me how my service and care for others in need is truly service and care for You. With every good thing I do to help someone else, I grow closer to You. Thank You for such wonderful purpose in my life. Please help me to simplify my life and to focus on the good things You have planned for me to do. Amen.

POWERFUL PRAYER

Read MATTHEW 6:5–13; LUKE 11:1–13; JOHN 17

Key Verse:

> Once Jesus was in a certain place praying.
> As he finished, one of his disciples came to
> him and said, "Lord, teach us to pray."
> LUKE 11:1 NLT

Understand:

* What most impacts you about how Jesus taught others to pray?

* What most impacts you from Jesus' prayer in John 17?

Apply:

In times of stress, when we feel like we just aren't sure how and what to pray, we can take a deep breath and go straight to the words of Jesus when He said, "This is how you should pray." Sometimes a bullet point list is helpful to follow when our minds feel scattered and unable to focus.

* Begin with praise to the Father.

* Ask for God's kingdom to come and His will to be done.

* Ask God to provide for daily needs without worry for needs of the future.

* Ask for forgiveness of sin and for help in extending forgiveness to others.

* Ask for protection from temptation and deliverance from evil.

We can apply the prayer that Jesus Himself instructed to every situation and need in our lives and the lives of our loved ones for whom we are praying.

Pray:

Loving Savior, I know I can pray to You about anything and everything, but please also help me keep good perspective and not overcomplicate my prayers, especially during stressful times. Bring me peace with the simplicity yet power of the way You have taught and have shown me how to pray in Your Word. Amen.

YOU ARE CONFIDENT IN HOPE

Read EPHESIANS 1:15–23

Key Verse:

> *I pray that your hearts will be flooded with light
> so that you can understand the confident hope
> he has given to those he called—his holy people
> who are his rich and glorious inheritance.*
> EPHESIANS 1:18 NLT

Understand:

- ✷ How does knowing that God calls you His child give you confident hope?

- ✷ What does it mean that you are God's rich and glorious inheritance?

- ✷ Where do you need God's power to be evident in your life today?

Apply:

Where light shines brightly, you can be confident in your next step. You don't fear unseen obstacles or holes to fall into. You can see your surroundings as they are and not wonder what's really out there. That kind of bright light is what Paul is praying illuminates the hearts of the believers in Ephesus—light that leads them to greater understanding, spiritual wisdom, and confident hope in today, tomorrow, and forever.

The hope we have through God's grace is not a mystical, vague feeling that everything will be okay. Our confident hope is a complete, steadfast understanding that we will be victorious through God. This certainty comes to us through the Holy Spirit who works in us.

Just as the sun rises this morning, ask God to flood your heart with His light. He will give you confident hope as you face today's challenges. You've got this because God's got this.

Pray:

Jesus, You are the Light of the world. Shine on me today.
Holy Spirit, You are my helper. Move in my heart today.
God, You are my mighty defender. Walk ahead of me today
and be victorious over the struggles and frustrations
and roadblocks that inevitably come my way. Amen.

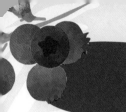

PRACTICE SECRET BLESSINGS

Read MATTHEW 6:1–4

Key Verses:

> "But when you give to the needy, do not let your left
> hand know what your right hand is doing, so that
> your giving may be in secret. Then your Father,
> who sees what is done in secret, will reward you."
> MATTHEW 6:3–4 NIV

Understand:

* Have you ever received a blessing in secret? How was it different from if you'd known who was behind the giving?

* Aside from God's promise of rewarding your secret generosity, why is giving in secret appealing?

* How can you meet a need in secret today?

Apply:

Pleasant surprises are one of life's greatest gifts. Whether you're on the giving or receiving end, a generous surprise that fills a need can buoy a spirit, turn a bad day into the best one, and even be a turning point in someone's life.

But God, in His wisdom, knows that when we give publicly—in a way that proclaims our goodness and generosity—it has a way of puffing up our pride. It feels good to be appreciated after all! If we're not careful, we're setting ourselves up to be praised above the one who is the giver of all good things.

That's why He asks us to give in secret. Give anonymously. Give with a thankful heart, hopeful that the recipient directs all gratitude to the great provider as well. Even though others don't see you, He sees you, and that's what's important.

Pray:

Generous God, thank You for the ability to give to others— to meet real needs in Your name. Show me opportunities to give in secret, and keep my motives pure so that I'm not seeking praise or glory for myself. Everything I have is from You, Father. I am so blessed. Amen.

THE GREATEST OF THESE IS LOVE

Read 1 Corinthians 13

Key Verse:

> *So these three things continue forever: faith, hope,*
> *and love. And the greatest of these is love.*
> 1 Corinthians 13:13 ncv

Understand:

* Why do you suppose God went to the trouble to let us know that love is greater than any other trait we might have?

* When God says that faith, hope, and love continue forever, what does He mean?

Apply:

Perhaps there is no chapter in the Bible quoted more often than the Love Chapter. You hear 1 Corinthians 13 most often at weddings. Love is the greatest of all the gifts. We read that, nod, and say, "Sure. I get it." But do we?

If love supersedes all, then we have to share it, even when we don't feel like it. When the neighbor's dog digs a hole under the fence. . .again. When the woman in the parking lot rams into your car. When the clerk at the supermarket double charges you for something but doesn't want to make it right.

Love has to show up in every relationship, every encounter, every disagreement, every bump in the road. When you offer it to others, you're truly offering them the greatest gift.

Is love leading the way in your life today?

Pray:

Lord, thank You for the reminder that love needs to lead the way. So often, I let my emotions get the best of me. I struggle to show love. When I don't feel it, Father, will You please love through me? Only then can I be a true reflection of You. Amen.

GOOD FRUIT

Read GALATIANS 5:13–26

Key Verses:

> But the fruit of the Spirit is love, joy, peace, forbearance,
> kindness, goodness, faithfulness, gentleness and
> self-control. Against such things there is no law.
> GALATIANS 5:22–23 NIV

Understand:

* Are there any fruits lacking in your life? How can you remedy that?

* When you're anxious or upset, which fruits are most beneficial to you, and why?

Apply:

Have you ever wondered why the various fruits of the Spirit are called "fruit" in the first place? Perhaps it's because a fruit is something sweet that is produced when the vine is healthy. If you have a healthy orange tree, you'll yield a healthy crop of oranges. If your grapevine is robust, there will be juicy grapes attached.

The same is true in your life. If you stay close to your

Creator, rooted and grounded in Him, your spiritual life will be healthy and robust. You'll begin to produce fruit for all to enjoy—love, joy, peace, forbearance, kindness, goodness, faithfulness, gentleness, and self-control. You won't have to summon these up; they will come as a natural result of spending time with your Savior.

So prepare yourself for a fruity future! Brace yourself for days filled with love for others, joy even in the midst of sorrow, unexplainable peace even when things are going wrong, patience with even the most annoying customer at work, and gentleness with your kiddos. God can do all this and more when you stick close to Him.

Pray:

Father, thank You for the reminder that I can see good results when I stick close to You. I want to bear fruit in my life so that I can be a good witness to others. Help me, I pray. Amen.

A FRESH START

Read LAMENTATIONS 3:22–33

Key Verses:

> *Because of the LORD's great love we are not consumed,*
> *for his compassions never fail. They are new*
> *every morning; great is your faithfulness.*
> LAMENTATIONS 3:22–23 NIV

Understand:

* What comfort do you take knowing that God's compassion doesn't run out?

* Why do you think morning is a good time to seek God's forgiveness?

* Who in your life needs to receive daily mercy from you (whether they ask for it or not)?

Apply:

Yesterday is done, and you messed it up again. You snapped at your kids and husband. You told that little fib at work. Through a lens of green, you saw the neighbors' new SUV and slammed the door of your junky vehicle a little harder than necessary. You told yourself you'll never be good enough, so why even try?

Yesterday felt like a train wreck, but this morning is a new day, and your Father God is here. He's saying, "Let's start again."

The truth is that God's forgiveness is available to us any hour of the day. He is faithful to show mercy whenever we ask Him for help. But time spent with our Father in the morning will result in a clear focus, renewed hope, and a greater understanding of our worth in Christ. It sets the day into motion in the best way possible.

Pray:

Merciful Father, this morning I seek Your refreshing forgiveness. I had every intention of perfection yesterday, but I messed up again. I'm ashamed of my sin, but I'm choosing to look up to You and admit I need Your kind compassion every day. I dedicate this new day to You, God. And I will live it as Your imperfect child who is perfectly loved by You. Amen.

YOU ARE LOVED

Read ROMANS 8:1–39

Key Verses:

> But in all these things we overwhelmingly conquer through
> Him who loved us. For I am convinced that neither death,
> nor life, nor angels, nor principalities, nor things present,
> nor things to come, nor powers, nor height, nor depth,
> nor any other created thing, will be able to separate us
> from the love of God, which is in Christ Jesus our Lord.
> ROMANS 8:37–39 NASB

Understand:

* What can separate the Christian from God's love?

* What does it mean that you are more than a conqueror
  in all things through Christ?

Apply:

Unconditionally—that is how God loves His children. These
verses in Romans provide the Christian with a great deal of
peace. Even death is not able to separate you from God's love.
Why is this? You will not truly experience death. You have
eternal life. To be absent in your current body is to be in the

presence of the Lord. So even the moment that you take your final breath on this earth you will not be separated from God!

As you go about your day, remember that God's love surrounds you. He has declared you to be more than a conqueror through Jesus. In other words, in all things—trials, tests, hardships, and even your deepest loss or disappointment—you have the power to overcome.

You are an overcomer, and you are deeply loved. Claim the scripture and walk with your head held high as a daughter of the King.

Pray:

Heavenly Father, Your Word is so rich and full of assurances. Help me to claim them! Thank You for loving me unconditionally and making me more than a conqueror over all things. In Jesus' powerful name I pray. Amen.

A SOUND MIND

Read LUKE 4:1–13

Key Verse:

> *When the devil had ended every temptation,*
> *he departed from him until an opportune time.*
> LUKE 4:13 ESV

Understand:

* Think of a time when the enemy reared his head against you. Did you fall for his lies?

* When you're tempted to give in to the enemy's tactics, what can you do to turn things around?

Apply:

If you read the opening lines of this story, you'll learn a lot: Jesus was full of the Holy Spirit and led by the Holy Spirit into the wilderness. When you submit yourself to the Spirit of God, when you say, "I'll let You be the one to lead and guide me," then you're always in a safe place.

Like Jesus, we will go through seasons of temptation. The enemy will do everything in his power to veer us off in the wrong direction. We might even wonder why or how we got to a place of confusion.

But when we're full of the Spirit of God, when we're completely and wholly submitted to the process of learning all we can learn, we have to trust that God is still in control, even when we're in the middle of the wilderness.

Where are you today? Feeling a little lost? Wondering how you got there? Instead of questioning the Lord or letting anxieties get the best of you, ask the Spirit of God to fill you to the top. He will guide you exactly where you need to go.

Pray:

> *I know that the safest place to be, Lord, is where Your Spirit guides me. Fill me today, I pray, and lead me where You will. I will gladly follow. Amen.*

AVOIDING GOSSIP

Read PROVERBS 26:17–28

Key Verse:

> *Fire goes out without wood, and quarrels*
> *disappear when gossip stops.*
> PROVERBS 26:20 NLT

Understand:

* Do you find gossip hard to avoid? Why or why not?

* Have you ever been the subject of gossip? How did it make you feel when you found out?

* The Bible uses the metaphor of fire for our tongue and destructive words we speak. What do words and fire have in common?

Apply:

Proverbs 26 is chock-full of relational wisdom. From the pitfalls of lying and butting into others' disagreements to warnings against flattery and smooth talking, the overarching message of this chapter is clear: it's often best to mind your own business.

Engaging in gossip—talking about others behind their

back—is the epitome of *not* minding your own business, and it can lead to misunderstanding, broken trust, and damaged relationships. Ah, but those bits of newsy gossip are so delicious, aren't they? Verse 22 (NLT) describes rumors as "dainty morsels that sink deep into one's heart" for good reason.

If you've developed an appetite for gossip, sometimes the easiest and simplest way to kick the habit is to avoid conversations with the person or people who are gossiping. If that's not possible, ask God for the wisdom to tell the others nibbling at the rumor morsels with you that you will no longer engage in it.

Pray:

Father, I never meant to gossip. It started out innocent enough. A "concern" of a mutual friend masqueraded as a prayer request, and it grew from there. Now feelings are hurt, and I feel terrible. So, I will keep my mouth shut, and Your Word says the fighting will disappear. I'm holding tightly to that truth, God! Amen.

POWER AND AUTHORITY

Read LUKE 9:1–17

Key Verses:

> *When Jesus had called the Twelve together, he gave*
> *them power and authority to drive out all demons and*
> *to cure diseases, and he sent them out to proclaim*
> *the kingdom of God and to heal the sick.*
> LUKE 9:1–2 NIV

Understand:

* God has given you authority, just as He gave the disciples. What's the most amazing thing you've witnessed as you've used this authority?

* Have you ever prayed for a sick person and watched that person be healed?

Apply:

Can you even imagine what the disciples must have been thinking as Jesus spoke words of power and authority over them? Picture yourself in their shoes, with the King of the universe looking you in the eye and saying, "I give you all power and authority to perform miracles, to drive out demons, to cure diseases, and to proclaim the gospel message!"

Wow! That will certainly push your anxieties and fears aside, won't it?

Here's the truth: Jesus has spoken those very same words over you. You have that same authority to speak life into situations, to pray over impossible circumstances, and to witness miracles. You have the power to preach the gospel, to share the love of Jesus with the unsaved, and to help those who are caught up in addiction.

Begin to claim that authority. Walk it out. Speak with faith and confidence as you pray in Jesus' name. Then, brace yourself! Miracles are surely on their way.

Pray:

> *I'm so grateful for Your authority, Jesus! When I speak*
> *in Your name, my words carry a lot of weight.*
> *Like the disciples, I will make a difference in*
> *my world. Thank You, Lord. Amen.*

GOD'S STRENGTH

Read ISAIAH 40

Key Verse:

> *He gives power to the weak and strength to the powerless.*
> ISAIAH 40:29 NLT

Understand:

* Isaiah 40 makes many statements about God. Which one grabs your attention? Why?

* What in this fallen world regularly drains you of strength and power?

Apply:

The prophet Isaiah asks the reader to consider who can be compared to God. He reminds us that God places the stars in the sky and knows them by name. He points out the greatness of God, saying that all the nations are like a grain of sand in God's hand.

In today's key verse, we see that power and strength are gifts from God. God, who is full of power, gifts His children with power. He is the source. We need only to tap into that source in order to be filled with strength.

What drains you? Is it work? A dysfunctional relationship? Caring for your family? Old wounds that never seem to fully heal? Whatever zaps you of your strength, lay it down and ask God to fill you with power. He longs to see you thriving again! Just as the children's song says: "I am weak, but He is strong. Yes, Jesus loves me."

Pray:

*Jesus, I am weak, but You are strong. You are powerful,
and I need some of that power to make it through the day.
Bless me, I pray. Fill me with strength to face this fallen
world with confidence and grit. I need You every hour!
Thank You for the power source that You are to my life. Amen.*

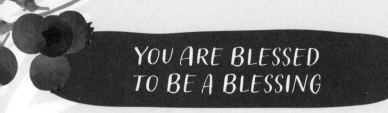

YOU ARE BLESSED TO BE A BLESSING

Read 2 Corinthians 9:6–15

Key Verse:

> *You will be enriched in every way so that you can be generous on every occasion, and through us your generosity will result in thanksgiving to God.*
> 2 Corinthians 9:11 niv

Understand:

* Why does God bless you?

* When have you been the recipient of someone's generosity? What did it mean to you?

* What needs can you meet today?

Apply:

We ask for and eagerly welcome God's blessings in our lives—food, shelter, clothing, money, to name a few—but why does God provide us with these things? One reason is that He enjoys giving good gifts to His children (see Matthew 7:11 and James 1:17), but another reason explained in 2 Corinthians 9 is that God blesses us so we can be a blessing to others.

Think of it! God gives us the opportunity to pay forward

the good gifts He gives to us. He invites us to follow His example and give generously, which not only blesses the receiver but also enriches our lives and results in praise and thanks to God!

Be on the lookout for ways to be generous with your time, talent, and money. And in the meantime, prepare to be generous. Make time to do it. Save money to do it. God is blessing you—to be a blessing!

Pray:

Lord God, You are so good to me! Today I am not taking for granted everything You give to me. I am so blessed! Show me where You want me to be generous today. Keep my motives pure and my eyes open to Your will. My desire is for Your blessings to not stop here but flow through me. Amen.

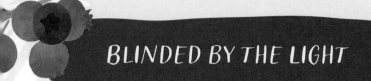

BLINDED BY THE LIGHT

Read ACTS 9:1–9

Key Verses:

> As he journeyed he came near Damascus,
> and suddenly a light shone around him from heaven.
> Then he fell to the ground, and heard a voice saying
> to him, "Saul, Saul, why are you persecuting Me?"
> ACTS 9:3–4 NKJV

Understand:

* Saul was moving in one direction in his life and then suddenly. . .bam! God stopped him in his tracks and turned his story around. Have you ever had an abrupt change like that?

* Have you known any Sauls, people whose lives were radically transformed?

Apply:

So many Bible stories (like this one) begin with a person having an ordinary day, doing an ordinary thing. Saul was just walking down the road, something he'd done hundreds of times before. Then, before he knew what hit him, a bright light blinded him and put a halt to his journey.

Saul's loss of vision was just the first of many things that would happen. God spoke very clearly to him and completely shifted his life journey. No longer would he be Saul the persecutor. He would be Paul the evangelist, who would change the course of history and whose name would be known thousands of years later.

Sometimes we have to be blinded in order to see. Maybe you've been there. God had to distract you with a supernatural experience to get your attention. Regardless of His tactic, the Lord has one goal in mind—to put you on the road that will lead to heaven.

Pray:

Lord, I don't want You to have to intervene in
my life in a supernatural way to get my attention.
May I be focused on You and moving in the direction
You want me to go. Today I recommit my life to
You, Jesus. May I only ever follow You. Amen.

GOOD WORKS PLANNED IN ADVANCE

Read EPHESIANS 2

Key Verse:

> *God has made us what we are. In Christ Jesus,*
> *God made us to do good works, which God planned*
> *in advance for us to live our lives doing.*
> EPHESIANS 2:10 NCV

Understand:

* How does Ephesians 2:8–9 say that a believer is saved?

* Ephesians 2:10 states that God planned in advance good works for us to do. What have you done in the past year to bring glory to God? The past month? The past week? Today?

Apply:

How amazing to think that God was making plans for us in advance! The good works that we take part in are part of His design. We are to live our lives bringing glory to our Creator. One way that we do this is through good deeds.

As you go through life, stop to take inventory of your gifts and passions. Talents and preferences were put in you by the one who knit you together in your mother's womb (see Psalm 139:13). When you use them, it doesn't feel like work because you are in your element. You are serving and giving and doing good deeds in your areas of strength.

You may not consider small acts significant, but they are important to God. The Bible mentions that if you even offer someone a cup of cold water, you are doing it unto Him (see Matthew 10:42). What small act will you do today that brings honor to the Father?

Pray:

Lord, it's dangerous to pray for opportunities, because then I know You will provide them! I long to serve You and please You through my good works. Show me what good works You planned for me in advance so that I might bring glory to You, my God. Amen.

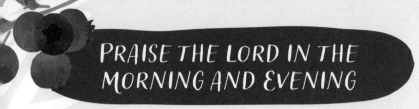

PRAISE THE LORD IN THE MORNING AND EVENING

Read PSALM 92

Key Verses:

> *It is good to praise the LORD and make music to your name, O Most High, proclaiming your love in the morning and your faithfulness at night.*
> PSALM 92:1–2 NIV

Understand:

* What do you do in the morning to intentionally set the tone for your day?

* Why do you think the psalm writer suggests that we proclaim God's love in the morning?

* ...and His faithfulness at night?

Apply:

For even the most spontaneous, schedule-adverse person, everyone has certain life rhythms. We live by the rising and setting of the sun; we have bookends to each day. This beginning and end is the perfect time to reset our hearts to align with God.

Psalm 92 tells us that it's good to praise the Lord in the

morning and celebrate His love. Why? Because throughout the day the world will beat us down with messages that we are unworthy, unqualified, unloved. And starting out the day rooted in the unending love of God will keep us standing strong.

The psalm writer then goes on to tell us to praise God at night and focus on His faithfulness. Why? Because God showed up throughout the day—in big ways and in small. He kept us going during moments of stress and anxiety, and He kept His promises. Reminding ourselves of His faithfulness helps us remember His unending goodness the next time we're struggling.

Praise Him this morning. Live in His love and faithfulness.

Pray:

God of love, thank You for lavishing Your care and devotion on me. I am made whole in Your love this morning. When I'm feeling unloved, unworthy, and forgotten today, wrap Your arms around me and remind me that I am Yours. Amen.

OUR SOURCE OF ALL COMFORT

Read 2 Corinthians 1

Key Verses:

> *All praise to God, the Father of our Lord Jesus Christ.*
> *God is our merciful Father and the source of all comfort.*
> *He comforts us in all our troubles so that we can*
> *comfort others. When they are troubled, we will be able*
> *to give them the same comfort God has given us.*
> 2 Corinthians 1:3–4 nlt

Understand:

* Have you ever felt crushed and overwhelmed beyond your ability to endure (verse 8)? How did God rescue you and comfort you?

* Can you say with confidence and a clear conscience that you have lived with a God-given holiness and sincerity in all your dealings (verse 12)?

Apply:

When you're all tucked in for the night, thank God for that cozy feeling, because it's a gift from Him. Yes, it might also come from your favorite soft pajamas and your pillows positioned just right, but ultimately even those are from God. The apostle Paul calls God the source of all comfort. Every bit of goodness you receive that eases your distress or weariness in any way is given by God to encourage, strengthen, and refresh you. And it doesn't stop with you. God calls you to share that comfort with others—maybe even with gifts like pj's and pillows but most importantly with the encouragement and peace that God filled you with at just the right time. Maybe your com fort came through a scripture God brought to mind on a really bad day or a straight-to-your-heart sermon on the radio when you were stuck in traffic. Maybe it came through a worship song repeated throughout your week or a friend who brought you coffee and cried and prayed with you. God shares His comfort in a zillion ways, both big and small. As you receive it, praise Him with gratitude and then spread it around generously.

Pray:

> *Heavenly Father, I think back on this day and see the many ways You provided comfort to me when I needed it. Thank You for providing the dear people and the precious gifts that encourage, refresh, and comfort me. Help me to generously pass them on. Amen.*

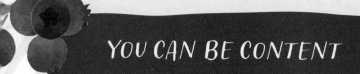

YOU CAN BE CONTENT

Read PHILIPPIANS 4:10–20

Key Verses:

> I know how to live on almost nothing or with everything.
> I have learned the secret of living in every situation, whether
> it is with a full stomach or empty, with plenty or little. For I
> can do everything through Christ, who gives me strength.
> PHILIPPIANS 4:12–13 NLT

Understand:

* In what areas of your life are you most content? Why?

* In what areas of your life are you most discontent?
  Why?

Apply:

Contentment is one of those virtues that the world almost entirely dismisses. Why should anyone be content when there's always more to be had? More wealth, more power, more status, better toys, bigger houses, newer technology, latest trends. But all that striving leaves us exhausted, frustrated, and discontent in heart and mind.

So, what's the best way to practice contentment? Start

with an attitude of thankfulness. When you take stock in the ways God provides for you, when you praise Him for all He's done, your heart will learn the secret to living satisfied and grateful in any situation. God will give you the strength and the untold peace that can only be found in Him.

Contentment doesn't come naturally to many of us, so start this morning by being intentional in thanking God. When you focus on His goodness, the world's shouted messages of "More, more, more!" will become nothing but background noise.

Pray:

God, I admit that I struggle with being content. My selfishness always seems to compare my situation with someone who has a little bit more. Forgive me for being ungrateful for all You provide. Teach me to be content in any situation, and if ends aren't meeting, give me the faith to trust that You will provide. Because I know You will. Amen.

WHILE WE WERE YET SINNERS

Read ROMANS 5

Key Verse:

> But God showed his great love for us by sending
> Christ to die for us while we were still sinners.
> ROMANS 5:8 NLT

Understand:

* What state were you in when Christ died for you?

* Do you ever feel like you need to clean up your act
  before you can talk to God? Is this accurate?

Apply:

Christ died for us while we were yet sinners. In other words,
He did not wait for us to straighten up and clean up and fess
up and do better. We couldn't. We were incapable of living any
other way until we met Him. We could not be "better enough"
to come before a holy God. We were full of sin and we were in
a heap of trouble. We needed salvation. And Jesus rescued us.

Remember this the next time you feel too guilty to talk to
Jesus, too dirty to come into His presence, or too ashamed to
pray. Jesus Christ went to the cross and took on all your sin.

He bore the weight of the sin of the entire world. He carried His cross to Calvary. He willingly died while we were yet sinners. There was no other way. It was God's plan from the beginning to redeem His people from sin.

Pray:

Thank You, Jesus. Thank You from the bottom of my heart for dying for me while I was still neck deep in sin. You did not wait for me to clean up my act. You cleaned it up. You, who had never sinned, took on my sin. You paid a debt You did not owe. I am eternally grateful. Amen.

GOD KNOWS YOUR NAME

Read Isaiah 43:1–13

Key Verse:

> *"Do not be afraid, for I have ransomed you.
> I have called you by name; you are mine."*
> Isaiah 43:1 nlt

Understand:

* What does the fact that God calls each of us by name tell you about Him?

* How does God demonstrate to you that you are precious to Him?

* Whom can you encourage today by reminding them that God knows their name?

Apply:

As small children, we instinctually give names to the possessions and people dearest to us. From a name for a beloved toy or a pet to a loving nickname for a sibling or a grandparent, putting our own label on something seems to say, "I've claimed you. You are mine."

God does the same for us, His cherished children. He

doesn't merely group us all together and love us as a mass of humanity. No, our Father God calls us *each* by name. He promises to be with *each* of us when we are going through difficulties. He has ransomed *each* of us and claimed *each* of us as His prized possession.

Our Creator knew us before He formed us. Before our parents imagined our names, He knew us and claimed us. Listen for His voice as He whispers your name today, and know that your identity is in Him.

Pray:

God, when I read Isaiah 43, I am overwhelmed by Your kindness to me. You tell me I am precious to You and You love me. You remind me again and again that You are with me no matter what and that I have nothing to fear. Forgive me when I forget these truths. Write them on my heart so I will always find my security in You. Amen.

THE WAIT IS ON

Read ACTS 1

Key Verses:

Once when he was eating with them, he told them not to leave Jerusalem. He said, "Wait here to receive the promise from the Father which I told you about. John baptized people with water, but in a few days you will be baptized with the Holy Spirit."

ACTS 1:4–5 NCV

Understand:

* Jesus instructed His followers to wait on the promise of the Holy Spirit. Has God ever asked you to wait on a particular promise? Are you good at waiting?

* The disciples were "in one accord" on the day of Pentecost. What is the importance of being in one accord with fellow believers as you wait on God to move in a miraculous way?

Apply:

Wait. Oh, how we hate that word. In this modern age, everything is instant, from popcorn to fast food to social media posts. Even our cars come with buttons to turn them on before we get inside. We don't want to wait on a thing.

Need that check deposited in the bank quickly? Do a mobile deposit. Need to sign a document to buy a home? E-sign it. Need a recommendation for a plumber? You'll find one online in seconds. Pretty much anything you need is at your fingertips.

Because we've gotten used to the notion that things should be instant, we forget that God often calls us to wait. Like the disciples in Jerusalem, we have to tarry. It's not just a matter of physically waiting. We must change our thinking. Instead of demanding instant gratification from God, we should praise Him during the waiting period.

What are you waiting on right now? Do you have a sense of urgency? If so, relax. Let those anxieties go. God's got this. The wait will be behind you soon. In the meantime, be found faithful.

Pray:

Lord, I'm sorry for my impatience! I've been demanding with You in the past, but those days are behind me now. I want to be found faithful in the waiting, Father. Help me, I pray. Amen.

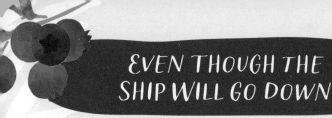

EVEN THOUGH THE SHIP WILL GO DOWN

Read ACTS 27:18–28:2

Key Verses:

> "But take courage! None of you will lose your lives, even though the ship will go down. For last night an angel of the God to whom I belong and whom I serve stood beside me, and he said, 'Don't be afraid, Paul. . . . God in his goodness has granted safety to everyone sailing with you.'"
> ACTS 27:22–24 NLT

Understand:

* What stresses in life make you feel like your ship is going down? Have you experienced a total shipwreck? How did you see God rescue and provide?

* How has God brought you the most peace and encouragement to keep you moving forward after a big failure in life?

Apply:

Paul was a prisoner on a ship in a horrible storm, and his words to the crew and other passengers were somewhat comforting but very unsettling too. We might wonder, *Why didn't God just stop the storm? Why let them shipwreck at all?* But we must remember that God has never promised to always protect us from shipwrecks—literal or figurative. Yet even in the midst of them, He can save our earthly lives. And what He does promise is heavenly life forever when we trust in Jesus as our one and only Savior. Just as God promised, eventually Paul and everyone on board the ship were safe. And we see how God provided for their needs through the good people of the island they landed on. This account helps give us peace when we feel our own ships are going down. Even when they do, God will always provide the people and resources we need to survive, and then He will lead us on a new course according to His will.

Pray:

Heavenly Father, I don't always understand why we have to endure "shipwrecks" in our lives. But I know You rescue according to Your will and ultimately save and give forever life to everyone who believes in Your Son. Thank You for always providing for my needs and bringing me aid in every hard situation. Amen.

THERE'S MORE THAN THIS

Read REVELATION 21:1–8

Key Verse:

"He will wipe away every tear from their eyes, and death shall be no more, neither shall there be mourning, nor crying, nor pain anymore, for the former things have passed away."
REVELATION 21:4 ESV

Understand:

* How does knowing there is something more after this life help you face today?

* What is one way you imagine heaven might be like?

* How might your relationship with God be different when you are fully present with Him in eternity?

Apply:

This old earth is broken and full of sadness. Stresses pile up and frustrations mount. Loss leaves us reeling, and pain is inevitable. In seasons when it feels like Murphy's Law reigns, we begin to wonder if the hurting will ever stop.

Revelation 21:4 is an encouraging Bible promise that we can cling to during the darkest times. Eternity for Christians includes a new heaven, a new earth, and a new reality that we simply cannot comprehend. No tears. No death or mourning or crying or pain.

Even better—God will make His home with us. He will dwell among us, closer than a next-door neighbor. We will have unbridled access to Him and all His goodness and mercy and love and abundance.

No one can say for certain what heaven will be like, but imagine what amazing things lie in store. And praise God for them.

Pray:

Heavenly Father, I am so thankful for the confidence I have in an eternity with You. I can't fathom the wonders that Your creative hand has in store for the new heaven and the new earth, and I can't wait to see Your masterful work! I long for that renewal personally too. Make me new today; change me to be more like You. Amen.

SIMPLE ACTS OF KINDNESS

Read 2 KINGS 4

Key Verses:

> The woman said to her husband, "I know that this is a
> holy man of God who passes by our house all the time.
> Let's make a small room on the roof and put a bed in the
> room for him. We can put a table, a chair, and a lampstand
> there. Then when he comes by, he can stay there."
>
> 2 KINGS 4:9–10 NCV

Understand:

* Have you gone out of your way to show hospitality to
  someone?

* Has someone ever been particularly kind to you? How
  did it make you feel?

Apply:

The Shunammite woman saw a need and wanted to meet
it. She recognized that Elisha was a holy man of God. She
proposed to her husband that rather than just feeding him
a meal each time he passed their way, they should provide
a room for him in their home. Isn't it kind how she planned

the details? She decided that a table, chair, and lampstand in addition to the bed would go into the small room on the roof for Elisha.

This simple act of kindness and hospitality was not done for a reward. The woman did not ask for anything in return. But, amazingly, she was granted a son because of her gesture.

When you see a need that you are able to meet, meet it. The most basic act of kindness can make all the difference in someone's life. And God sees your good deeds. If not in this life, you will find your reward in heaven. The Lord is pleased when we serve and love one another.

Pray:

Lord, all my resources come straight from Your hand. Nothing that I own—my home, my car, even the food in my pantry—belongs to me. It is all on loan from You. Please show me opportunities to use my resources to meet the needs of those around me. Make me hospitable and kind like the Shunammite woman. In Christ's name I pray. Amen.

THE VINE AND THE BRANCHES

Read JOHN 15

Key Verses:

"I am the true grapevine, and my Father is the gardener.
He cuts off every branch of mine that doesn't produce fruit,
and he prunes the branches that do bear fruit so they will
produce even more. You have already been pruned and
purified by the message I have given you. Remain in me,
and I will remain in you. For a branch cannot produce fruit
if it is severed from the vine, and you cannot be fruitful
unless you remain in me. Yes, I am the vine; you are the
branches. Those who remain in me, and I in them, will
produce much fruit. For apart from me you can do nothing."

JOHN 15:1–5 NLT

Understand:

* What good fruit are you producing in your life
  right now?

* What ways can you improve on staying connected to
  Jesus, the vine?

Apply:

Jesus described Himself as a vine and God the Father as the gardener. We are the branches. The fruits we grow on our branches are the good things we do for God that He has planned for us—the work He created us for, serving and giving to others, sharing God's love, and helping others to know Jesus as Savior. And we can't produce any good fruit unless we stay connected to Jesus, the vine. If you are feeling worn out and unproductive and like you're spinning your wheels at times, there might be an easy answer: you might need to check your connection to Jesus. Humbly ask the loving gardener to show you any problems and nourish you back to nearness with Jesus. God can make you thrive again with lots of good fruit growing on you!

Pray:

Heavenly Father, please nourish me in my connection to Jesus, the vine. Help me to stay connected and grow the good fruit You want me to. Amen.

WHEN HOPE IS GONE

Read ZECHARIAH 9:9–12

Key Verse:

> *Return to your fortress, you prisoners of hope; even now*
> *I announce that I will restore twice as much to you.*
> ZECHARIAH 9:12 NIV

Understand:

* When you feel hopeless, in what way are you a "prisoner of hope"? What might freedom mean for you?

* What do you think the fortress is that's referred to in the key verse? Can you think of "fortresses" in your own life where you might be able to return for safety?

Apply:

Sometimes life looks pretty hopeless. Whether we're facing a personal problem or considering the state of our world, the situation gives us little cause for hope. As hard as we try, we just can't see any solutions.

When that happens, we often become afraid to hope any longer. Because we've had our hopes dashed so often, hope becomes something painful. It seems like a prison, a trap that holds us back from facing reality, rather than something positive that gives us courage.

But the kind of hope the Bible talks about isn't merely wishing that things will turn out the way we want them to. Instead, it's a confident expectation that no matter how bad things look, God is behind the scenes working out something better than anything we could ever come up with on our own. The result may not be what we wished would happen—but ultimately, God tells us, it will be twice as good!

Pray:

God of hope, show me Your fortress where I will be safe during this time when it's so hard to hold on to hope. I'll stop looking for my own solutions and instead will wait for You to act. My hope is only in You. Amen.

THE ONE WHO LIVES IN YOU

Read 1 JOHN 4

Key Verse:

> *My children, you are a part of God's family. You have stood against these false preachers and had power over them. You had power over them because the One Who lives in you is stronger than the one who is in the world.*
>
> 1 JOHN 4:4 NLV

Understand:

* What does this passage say is the test for knowing what is truly from the Spirit of God?

* How do verses 16–18 speak comfort to any anxieties in your life right now?

Apply:

"The One Who lives in you is stronger than the one who is in the world"—that last part of 1 John 4:4 is such a short and simple yet powerful scripture to memorize and repeat when you need strength and courage in any situation. Our enemy the devil is the one stirring up all kinds of evil in this world. And you will be under attack from him sometimes, in all sorts of different ways—through stressful times for your family, through painful times of loss, through illness, and so on. But no matter how strong the enemy and his evil seem against you and your loved ones, he is never stronger than the power of God in you through the Holy Spirit. Don't ever forget that. Call on Him to help you be strong, calm, and patient and to help you see how He is working and taking care of you through it all.

Pray:

Heavenly Father, deep down I know You are always stronger than any evil attack against me, any hard thing I'm going through. But I do forget that truth sometimes, and I'm sorry. Please remind me, fill me with Your power and peace, and do the fighting for me. Amen.

LOVE DIFFICULT PEOPLE

Read LUKE 6:27–35

Key Verses:

> "I say to you who hear Me, love those who work against
> you. Do good to those who hate you. Respect and
> give thanks for those who try to bring bad to you.
> Pray for those who make it very hard for you."
> LUKE 6:27–28 NLV

Understand:

* Who is the most difficult person in your life, and what makes that person such a challenge?

* How, practically, can you do something good and show respect for this person today?

* How could your perspective change if you make it a priority to pray for this person?

Apply:

Most of us are conflict avoiders. Apart from those rare few who are wired to enjoy a good combative exchange, we intentionally structure our lives to be harmonious in whatever ways we can.

But there's always that person who is just so difficult. Maybe it's a coworker who seems to sabotage your efforts. Maybe it's an in-law who has never warmed to your presence in the family. Maybe it's someone who struggles socially, and it comes across as disrespect, creating awkward situations. Maybe it's simply someone who doesn't like you and makes no qualms about it.

Jesus says love them anyway. Do good to them. Respect them and pray for them. This might be one of Jesus' most challenging commands, yet He demonstrated it over and over in His ministry on earth. With His help, you can do it.

Pray:

This is a hard one, God. I receive no respect, so everything inside me wants to disrespect in return. And love them? Do good to them? I can't do this on my own, Father. Inhabit this relationship. Give me Your eyes to see them the way You see them. That's the only way I will be able to love. Amen.

PLEASANT AND PEACEFUL

Read PHILIPPIANS 2

Key Verses:

God is helping you obey Him. God is doing what He wants done in you. Be glad you can do the things you should be doing. Do all things without arguing and talking about how you wish you did not have to do them. In that way, you can prove yourselves to be without blame. You are God's children and no one can talk against you, even in a sin-loving and sin-sick world. You are to shine as lights among the sinful people of this world.
PHILIPPIANS 2:13–15 NLV

Understand:

* How does imitating Christ in His humility help fill you with peace?

* How does keeping a positive attitude, without grumbling or complaining, help fill you with peace?

Apply:

Yikes, it's terribly hard to do *all* things without ever arguing or complaining, isn't it? But that's what this scripture encourages us to do. It's something with which we all need a lot of help from God. But if we can keep positive with our words as we obey God and follow the plans He has for us, we shine as extra bright lights in the dark and sinful world around us. Hopefully, people who do not trust Jesus as their Savior will want to know more about God's love because they will see our lights shining in our pleasant and peaceful attitudes, no matter the situation.

Pray:

Heavenly Father, please help me to be an extraordinary light in the darkness of sin around me in this world. I want to shine so brightly that others want to know Jesus as their Savior too. Amen.

CONFIDENCE IN GOD

Read 1 SAMUEL 17

Key Verse:

> And David said, "The LORD who delivered me from the
> paw of the lion and from the paw of the bear, He will
> deliver me from the hand of this Philistine." And Saul
> said to David, "Go, and may the LORD be with you."
> 1 SAMUEL 17:37 NASB

Understand:

* What gave David the confidence to fight Goliath,
  the Philistine giant?

* What experiences have you had that give you
  confidence to face an unknown future with a
  known God?

Apply:

As a shepherd, David was to watch over the sheep. This
job entailed fighting off wild animals that intended to kill
the sheep. David had become skilled at his work. God had
protected him. He had not died from a bear or lion attack, and
for a shepherd, these were very real possibilities.

What David had faced in his past enabled him to face a new challenge with confidence. But notice this: It was not David's confidence in himself or in his own strength or ability that led him to fight the giant. It was his trust in the Lord.

"The Lord who delivered me" was the one David bragged on, not himself.

Look back in your life. Where has God protected or delivered you? God will use each of your experiences to prepare you for the next. Be prepared for a greater challenge that lies ahead.

Pray:

Lord, thank You for the times You have protected me and provided a way of escape. You have built up in me a confidence that next time and the time after that You will remain faithful. You will show up. Help me to trust in Your strength as You continue to use me and to put challenges in my path. Amen.

IN SPITE OF

Read JOB 1

Key Verse:

In all this Job did not sin or blame God.
JOB 1:22 NLV

Understand:

* Have you ever wanted to point the finger at God, to blame Him for the bad things happening in your life?
* Where is God when things are falling apart?

Apply:

In spite of everything, Job did not sin or blame God. Let those words sink in for a moment. In spite of pain. Sickness. Death. Loss. Destruction.

Us? We're so quick to blame. When a meal isn't right, we blame the cook or waitress. When our team doesn't win, we blame the umpire or referee. When we show up late for an event, we're loaded with excuses for how others slowed us down.

Pointing the finger is a natural defense, but maybe it's time to adopt Job's attitude. Even when he lost everything, he didn't point the finger at God. He could have. (Let's face it, most of us would.) He could have pointed to heaven and shouted, "Why are You doing this to me? What did I ever do to You?"

The truth is, even in the hardest of times, God wants us to keep our eyes fixed on Him and our hope elevated. So toss those anxieties out the window. Stop blaming. Keep your eyes on the one who plans to deliver you; then watch as He works all things together for your good.

Pray:

I needed that reminder today, Lord! I'm so quick to point the finger. Today I choose to adopt Job's stance and remind myself that, in spite of everything, You are still good. Amen.

YOU CAN LIVE WITHOUT FEAR

Read ISAIAH 41:8–14

Key Verses:

> "For I have chosen you and will not throw you away.
> Don't be afraid, for I am with you. Don't be discouraged,
> for I am your God. I will strengthen you and help you.
> I will hold you up with my victorious right hand."
> ISAIAH 41:9–10 NLT

Understand:

* Have you ever considered the fact that God will not throw you away? How does that fact make you feel?

* How can knowing God is with you make you less fearful? Less discouraged?

Apply:

Fear is something like a strain of influenza. Just when we think we've figured out the proper vaccine to safeguard ourselves, the virus changes, and the flu rears its ugly head once again. And just when we think we've overcome our fear, some new worry or anxiety pops up, and anxious thoughts return, sometimes leaving us down for the count.

The only true cure for fear is unconditional trust in God. Faith that He will keep His promises all throughout scripture. He has chosen you. He will not throw you away. He is with you. He is your God who will strengthen you and help you. He will hold you up.

Do you believe Him? When your fears threaten to take over again, remember His faithfulness in keeping these promises in the past. He has never failed you yet, and He will not start now.

Pray:

Almighty God, no matter what I face, I know You are with me. You chose me for a reason, and I know You have a perfect plan for me safe inside Your will. Be near me, Father, especially when I am feeling unsure of the way. Hold me up when I can't stand on my own, and usher me into Your victorious presence forevermore. Amen.

THE HEROES WHO HAVE GONE BEFORE US

Read HEBREWS 11

Key Verse:

> *They were longing for a better country—a heavenly one. Therefore God is not ashamed to be called their God, for he has prepared a city for them.*
> HEBREWS 11:16 NIV

Understand:

* Which of the faith heroes described in Hebrews 11 do you relate to the most?

* Do you feel like a foreigner and nomad here on earth? Why is that important?

Apply:

We have to admit, sometimes we do get weary of keeping the faith. We wonder why God isn't answering a specific prayer or creating the breakthrough we think we need or proving Himself exactly like we want Him to. We sometimes have doubt and need to be honest about it. In those times, Hebrews 11 is such a powerful chapter to read to revitalize you. It defines what our faith is—being sure of what we hope for and certain of what we do not see—and gives us an incredible overview of so many heroes who've gone before us holding to their faith. This reminds us and inspires us to keep on believing and being obedient to God, like they did, even when we can't see all His plans or the final result. If you are ever tempted to give up the faith, open your Bible to Hebrews 11. Read and reenergize. Think of how you'd like your name to be remembered among your family and friends and generations as one who never gave up on God. Though we cannot see all that He is doing right now, we absolutely will one day soon.

Pray:

Heavenly Father, please strengthen my faith in You as I remember the heroes of old who never gave up on You. Thank You for their examples in Your Word. Please remind me every day that I am looking to and living for a place far, far better than this world—the heavenly home where You make all things right and good. Amen.

NEVER ALONE

Read REVELATION 3

Key Verse:

> "Here I am! I stand at the door and knock. If anyone
> hears my voice and opens the door, I will come in
> and eat with that person, and they with me."
> REVELATION 3:20 NIV

Understand:

* If you are a believer in Christ, are you ever truly alone?

* Why do you think Jesus refers to eating with the person
  who allows Him into his heart?

Apply:

If you have Christ as your Savior, you are never truly alone.
On your darkest day and in your loneliest hour, He stands
ready to eat with you. Why would He use these words? One
might wonder if it's because eating a meal together is an
intimate act. We typically eat our meals as a family or with
close friends, not with strangers. We talk as we eat. It's a time
to slow down and spend time with loved ones. It's a shared
experience.

Even if there is no one else, there will always be Christ. He is your Savior and Redeemer, your friend, your Prince of Peace, and the King of Glory. He is always there for you. You are never truly alone.

Christ not only saves you but also promises to be with you always, never leaving or forsaking you. He comes in and makes His home with you. You are His beloved, and He longs to fellowship with you.

Pray:

Lord Jesus, thank You for coming into my heart. Thank You that I am never really alone because I have You. May I always recognize the great gift of my fellowship with You. Amen.

REBORN!

Read JOHN 3:1–21

Key Verse:

> *"You should not be surprised at my saying,*
> *'You must be born again.'"*
> JOHN 3:7 NIV

Understand:

* It's impossible to remember your own physical birth, but do you have a memory of the day you gave your heart to the Lord? What was that day like?

* When you explain the salvation process to others, do you share from your own journey? What do you say?

Apply:

Countless Bible stories tell tales of men and women who messed up and wanted to start over. Thank goodness God is in the do-over business. He loves to offer second chances.

There's one do-over that outshines every other, and it's found in one little word: *salvation*. When we accept Jesus Christ as Lord and Savior, when we step into relationship with Him, we are reborn.

Think about that prefix "re-" for a moment. It means "again." When we accept Jesus, we're born. . .again. We get a do-over. A big one! Gone are the mistakes of the past. Washed away are our sins. Gone are the worries about who we used to be. In place of all these things, a clean slate. What an amazing gift from our Father, God!

Pray:

Thank You, Lord, for offering me new life in You. I've been born again, Father! My heart now belongs to You. I can hardly wait to get started on this journey together. Amen.

A BETTER CHOICE

Read GENESIS 3

Key Verse:

>*When the woman saw that the tree was good for food, and that it was pleasant to the eyes, and a tree to be desired to make one wise, she took of the fruit thereof, and did eat, and gave also unto her husband with her; and he did eat.*
>GENESIS 3:6 KJV

Understand:

* Eve saw that the tree was good for food, so she took the fruit. . .even though God had told her not to. She let something that looked good outweigh God's best. Have you ever done that?

* When we deliberately choose to disobey, what are the consequences?

Apply:

Life is filled with choices. We make dozens of them a day. Will we get out of bed when the alarm goes off? What shoes will we wear today? What clothes? Should we eat breakfast or skip it? Do we drop off the kids at school or make them ride the bus?

Do we start the slow cooker before leaving for work or pick up fast food on the way home this evening?

These are just a few of the choices we make.

Of course, there are bigger choices too: Whom will we marry? How many children should we have? Where will we live?

The biggest choice we'll ever make, though, is far more important than any of these: Will we give our heart to Jesus Christ and make Him Lord of our life?

Following God is the best choice we could ever make. And listening to His voice as we move forward from day to day is critical for our survival. Eve wanted to walk in relationship with God in the garden, but she wanted to have it her way too. She made a poor choice, one that had devastating consequences for mankind. May we learn from her mistake so we're not destined to repeat it.

Pray:

> *Father, I want to make good choices! I long to have a solid relationship with You, so I'll listen for Your still, small voice. Give me clear instructions so that I can follow hard and fast after You, Lord. Amen.*

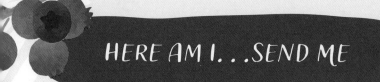

HERE AM I. . .SEND ME

Read ISAIAH 6:1–8

Key Verse:

> Then I heard the voice of the Lord, saying,
> "Whom shall I send, and who will go for Us?"
> Then I said, "Here am I. Send me!"
> ISAIAH 6:8 NASB

Understand:

* Can you remember a time in your life when the Lord specifically called you to go someplace out of your comfort zone? Did you hide in fear or respond, like Isaiah, "Here am I. Send me!"?

* When was the last time you felt the Lord nudge you to do something difficult or unusual?

Apply:

Isaiah found himself in an amazing position, didn't he? When the Lord asked the question "Whom shall I send, and who will go for Us?" Isaiah was faced with a choice—to stay or to go. With no hesitation, he responded, "Here am I. Send me!"

If you've ever spent time in God's presence, really drawing close to Him, perhaps you've had those little nudges. Maybe you've heard God whisper to your heart, "Go here" or "Do this" or "Do that." When the almighty author of the universe speaks, how do you respond? Ideally, like Isaiah!

If God reveals something to you during your quiet time with Him, don't be afraid. Simply raise your hand and say, "I'm here, Lord. I hear You, and I'm willing to go." But don't be surprised where He sends you once you've said it! Your journey is about to get really interesting!

Pray:

> *Lord, here am I. Send me. Send me to my friends, that I might be a witness. Send me to my coworkers, that I might show compassion. Send me wherever You choose, that I might shine brightly for You. Amen.*

RELY ON HIM

Read PSALM 33:16–22

Key Verses:

Don't count on your warhorse to give you victory—for all its strength, it cannot save you. But the LORD watches over those who fear him, those who rely on his unfailing love.
PSALM 33:17–18 NLT

Understand:

* Have you ever put your faith in someone or something that left you disappointed? What did you learn from that experience?

* How do you know you can trust God to take care of you?

Apply:

Scripture uses the beautiful shepherd/sheep analogy to describe our relationship with God. Passages like Psalm 23 can fill us with peace and security to know that He takes care of us no matter what.

But just like sheep, we sometimes make dumb choices about whom or what to trust. Ever been burned by the latest self-help craze? Has a friend or family member let you down? Maybe someone betrayed your trust after you shared something deeply personal. Quick fixes and three steps to a brand-new you can leave us feeling defeated, empty, and hopeless.

But our Good Shepherd is there, always seeking us, calling us back to Him. His love is unfailing, and His saving grace is absolute. Trust in Him to guide you, to protect you, to make your path clear for safe passage to eternity with Him.

Pray:

Thank You for watching over me, Father. You keep me safe and preserve my life in ways that I won't know this side of heaven. Your strength is what I put my trust in—not my own, not other people's. I am imperfect, and others will let me down whether they mean to or not. Your redeeming love lifts me up and holds me steady even in hard times. Amen.

MANNA

Read Exodus 16

Key Verse:

Then the Lord said to Moses, "I will rain down bread from heaven for you. The people are to go out each day and gather enough for that day. In this way I will test them and see whether they will follow my instructions."

Exodus 16:4 NIV

Understand:

* God is in the "providing" business. The Bible promises that He will take care of His kids. Think of a particular time when God came through for you, pouring down unexpected manna.

* How can you be a manna provider for others in need?

Apply:

We often say, "Lord, I don't need much. Just give me what I need, not what I want." Likely, the Israelites prayed that too. "Lord, just a little food will suffice to see us through." Then, manna fell like a feast from the sky. At first the Hebrew children were thrilled to have it. Then, after a while, it wasn't so tasty. They grew tired of it.

What an amazing story this would have been if the Israelites continued to praise and thank God for His provision instead of grumbling. If only they could have seen manna as a blessing instead of drudgery.

Maybe you can relate. What felt like a blessing in the beginning is now part of your everyday humdrum existence. You've forgotten to be thankful. The mortgage gets paid, and you don't remember to thank God. The electric bill is paid, and you let it pass by like it's nothing.

Every day God is blessing you. Don't forget to stop and thank Him for the manna!

Pray:

Lord, thank You for the many times and ways You have provided for me. Show me how to be a blessing to others, I pray. I want to be one who provides manna (refreshment, nourishment) to those You place in my path. Amen.

HE IS NEAR TO THE BROKENHEARTED

Read PSALM 34

Key Verses:

> The LORD is near to the brokenhearted and saves
> the crushed in spirit. Many are the afflictions of the
> righteous, but the LORD delivers him out of them all.
> PSALM 34:18–19 ESV

Understand:

* Do you feel the presence of God more during times of
  joy or times of sorrow? Why?

* Think about a time when you called out to God with a
  crushed spirit. How did He respond?

Apply:

God's Word doesn't promise a life of unbridled bliss for God's
children. On the contrary, Jesus tells us in John 16:33 (NLT),
"Here on earth you will have many trials and sorrows."

But God is near, and during life's toughest situations, He
will rescue us from despair. His path will guide us through
and give us the strength to overcome anything. Maybe you've
seen friends or family go through impossible things like this

and come out the other side stronger in their faith.

Yes, God will walk with us, carrying us when necessary, through life's many trials and sorrows. But the best news of all is what Jesus said in John 16, right after telling us to expect difficult times. "But take heart," He says in the second half of verse 33, "because I have overcome the world." Christ wins. We are victorious in Him.

Pray:

Lord of all my days, thank You for always being near. I love to celebrate with You when things are going well, but I am also deeply grateful that You come even closer when I am brokenhearted, grieving, and crushed in spirit. You are faithful to bring me through and are so patient with me when I am struggling. I don't deserve such kindness, but I am so thankful for it! Amen.

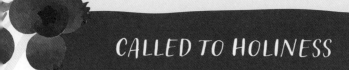

CALLED TO HOLINESS

Read 1 PETER 2

Key Verse:

> *People who do not believe are living all around you and might say that you are doing wrong. Live such good lives that they will see the good things you do and will give glory to God on the day when Christ comes again.*
> 1 PETER 2:12 NCV

Understand:

* Why should believers do good deeds? What is the purpose?

* What are you doing that points others to Christ?

Apply:

A major way that Christians stand out in the world is by living good lives and doing good things. The choices you make regarding clothing, entertainment, and how you spend your money are noticed by those around you. People know that you are a Christian, and when you live a good life before them, you point them to Christ.

It's hard to argue with good results. When people see your

children showing respect to others and making good choices, they will wonder what you are doing differently as a mother. When people notice that you support missions or give of your time to minister to others, they will wonder why.

One of the greatest ways to witness to those around you is by living a godly life before them. When others notice the difference in you, you can point them to Jesus. Our good deeds have one purpose—to bring glory to God.

Pray:

> *God, help me to live in such a way that others are drawn to You. I want everything I do and say to reflect the fact that I am a child of the King. Please help me to set a good example and to live above reproach so that others might glorify You, my Father in heaven. Amen.*

HONOR AND PRAISE FOREVER AND EVER

Read PSALMS 145–146

Key Verses:

> I will honor You every day, and praise Your name forever and ever. The Lord is great and our praise to Him should be great. He is too great for anyone to understand. Families of this time will praise Your works to the families-to-come.
>
> PSALM 145:2–4 NLV

Understand:

* Is verse 4 of this passage a goal in your family? Do you strive to praise God and His awesome works and inspire the next generation of your family to do the same?

* Do you think your praise to God is great? How could it be even greater?

Apply:

Tonight, let these psalms of praise be as soothing as a bedtime bubble bath. Focus your thoughts on your heavenly Father, and sing and pray the words of Psalms 145–146 to Him. Thank Him for all His mighty acts and kindnesses and for the ways He is slow to anger. Feel His closeness because He is "near to all who call on Him, to all who call on Him in truth" (Psalm 145:18 NLV). Trust that He takes care of you and will destroy the sinful. Do not put your ultimate trust in people who will fail you at times; rather, remember that God alone will never fail you, and your hope in Him is sure. He is your Creator, provider, healer, protector, deliverer, and your faithful and loving King! If you fill your mind with this kind of truth over and over, there is no room for worry or fear. Let your mind relax in the truth of God's Word, and enjoy sweet rest.

Pray:

Heavenly Father, You are so great that no one can fully understand it, but I want my praise to You to be great as well. I want my mind and my mouth to be full of constant praise to You and empty of worry and fear. Oh, how I love You, Lord! Amen.

YOU ARE RESILIENT

Read ZEPHANIAH 3:14–20

Key Verses:

> *"Do not fear, Zion; do not let your hands hang limp.*
> *The LORD your God is with you, the Mighty Warrior who*
> *saves. He will take great delight in you; in his love he will*
> *no longer rebuke you, but will rejoice over you with singing."*
> ZEPHANIAH 3:16–17 NIV

Understand:

* What challenge are you facing today that has your hands hanging limp?

* What makes you feel strong?

* How does it change your perspective when you realize that God, the Mighty Warrior who saves, is with you?

Apply:

Each single day brings its own challenges, but life often hurls difficult seasons at us. For days, weeks, months, or years, challenging times can leave us weary, can leave us afraid, and may even threaten to defeat us.

What are you facing today?

Take courage, for you are the daughter of the mighty Lord. Be confident in the fact that you are a resilient woman of God—not because of your own strength but because God, the King and Mighty Warrior who saves, is with you. He will not make fun of you for struggling in times of distress—He wants to love you, protect you, and fight with you through it. He takes delight in you and rejoices over you with singing! He is your rescuer and the reason you can overcome any challenge you face.

Praise Him for past victories and stand strong in Him today.

Pray:

Defender God, thank You for saving me. I praise You for the strength You instill in me. Today I will lift my head and raise my hands in Your victory even in the midst of my struggles. I delight in You, Father. Your ways are good and perfect, so please lead me today. Amen.

A PRAYER AND PROMISE

Read 1 SAMUEL 1

Key Verses:

> Hannah was in deep anguish, crying bitterly as she prayed
> to the LORD. And she made this vow: "O LORD of Heaven's
> Armies, if you will look upon my sorrow and answer my
> prayer and give me a son, then I will give him back to you.
> He will be yours for his entire lifetime, and as a sign that he
> has been dedicated to the LORD, his hair will never be cut."
>
> 1 SAMUEL 1:10–11 NLT

Understand:

* What was Eli's first response as he observed Hannah
  praying? Have you ever experienced something like
  that? How did that make you feel?

* How do you think Hannah must have felt as she
  followed through on her promise and took Samuel to
  the temple to live at such a young age? What does that
  say about her and her faith?

Apply:

Hannah knew what it felt like to think maybe God had forgotten or didn't care about her. Can you relate? Maybe you too are desperately praying for children right now, and God has not answered that desire. Or maybe you've been asking God to answer other requests to no avail. Whatever the case, don't give up. Let Hannah's story inspire you and give you peace tonight. She continued to pray for a son, and she showed her love and devotion to God by promising that if He agreed, she would let that son live at the temple to serve God his whole life. When God finally answered and blessed her with Samuel, Hannah followed through on her promise and was rewarded even more for her faithfulness. And Samuel grew to be a great prophet for God. He was a blessing to all the people of Israel because of Hannah's faithful prayer and promise.

Pray:

*Heavenly Father, please hear my requests and desires.
Please help them to match Your perfect will for me.
I promise to use my blessings to give back to You!
Please help me to always keep that promise. Amen.*

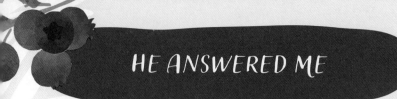

HE ANSWERED ME

Read GENESIS 21:1–21

Key Verses:

> *Now the LORD was gracious to Sarah as he had said,*
> *and the LORD did for Sarah what he had promised.*
> *Sarah became pregnant and bore a son to Abraham in*
> *his old age, at the very time God had promised him.*
> GENESIS 21:1–2 NIV

Understand:

* During anxious seasons, it's easy to give up. Have you ever had to persevere like Abraham and Sarah? What was the outcome of your perseverance?

* God moved in a miraculous way in Sarah's life. Have you ever experienced a miracle in your own life?

Apply:

Abraham and Sarah were elderly when their son, Isaac, was born. No wonder Sarah laughed when she learned she was having a child. Not many women in their golden years give birth to babies!

Isaac was the long-awaited promise, the child they'd

always longed for. His arrival was the culmination of many years of hoping, praying, and believing despite the odds.

Maybe you've been waiting a long time for something—a husband, a child, a new job, a home. You've pleaded with God, and it all seems to be in vain. You're nearly ready to give up. Circumstances have almost convinced you it's never going to happen.

Today, let your faith be invigorated again. Read through Abraham and Sarah's story and allow your heart to dream once more. God is a dream giver and a dream fulfiller. Allow Him to see this miracle all the way through.

Pray:

> *Father, thank You for the reminder that the dreams*
> *You've laid on my heart are God breathed and*
> *will be God fulfilled. I remove my hands and*
> *choose to trust You today, Lord. Amen.*

127

YOU CANNOT LOSE GOD'S LOVE

Read PSALM 136

Key Verse:

> *Give thanks to the God of heaven.*
> *His love endures forever.*
> PSALM 136:26 NIV

Understand:

* How does the fact that you cannot lose God's love affect your relationship with Him?

* Are you ever guarded in what you say to Him? Why or why not?

* How is God's love better than any other love?

Apply:

Psalm 136 repeats the phrase "His love endures forever" twenty-six times. It's as if the writer knows how easily we forget God's faithfulness, so after each statement, he reminds us (and himself), "His love endures forever."

The fact remains, if we are children of the God of heaven, we cannot lose His love. We are His forever—chosen, bought at a price, accepted, forgiven, redeemed, and a full heir to His kingdom.

Yet still we mess up, and doubt creeps in. We're not good enough. Not worthy of being forgiven for the same sin...again.

His love endures forever.

We worry and fret; anxious thoughts overtake us as we stumble through life. Forgetting that we've been saved and are protected by a mighty God, we try to fight our battles ourselves, sometimes pushing Him away.

His love endures forever.

You cannot lose His love, friend. Rest in that promise, and thank Him for His steadfastness today.

Pray:

Unending God, I see Your care for me everywhere. From the beauty of Your creation and the blessings You so generously lavish on me to the people You have placed in my life and the unique talents You have made in me, I feel Your love with every breath I take. Thank You for choosing me. Thank You for loving me always and forever. Amen.

ACCEPTING HELP

Read JAMES 2

Key Verses:

> *A brother or sister in Christ might need clothes or food.*
> *If you say to that person, "God be with you! I hope you*
> *stay warm and get plenty to eat," but you do not give what*
> *that person needs, your words are worth nothing.*
> JAMES 2:15–16 NCV

Understand:

* What is the difference between faith with and without works?

* Why do you think James says that faith without works is dead?

Apply:

God loves you. All of you. Not just the spiritual parts. He cares about your physical needs as well. The body of Christ should always be about helping one another.

At times you will need help. You may feel tempted to say, "It's okay, thanks anyway, but I've got this." It may be hard for you to accept help. You may feel that you can do it all in your own strength. This may seem strong. It may feel brave. But, in actuality, what you are doing is denying others the opportunity to help you. This denies them a great blessing.

Remember how good it felt last time you extended a helping hand to someone in need? Be sure that you are also allowing God's people to bless you in your own time of need.

Pray:

Lord, thank You for showing me that faith must involve works. I am saved by grace, but because of Your amazing grace, I am inspired to do good works so that others may come to know You. Help me also to be willing to accept help. In doing so, I allow others to live out their faith as well. In Jesus' name I pray. Amen.

POWERFUL PEP TALK

Read JOSHUA 1

Key Verses:

>"Study this Book of Instruction continually. Meditate on it day and night so you will be sure to obey everything written in it. Only then will you prosper and succeed in all you do. This is my command—be strong and courageous! Do not be afraid or discouraged. For the LORD your God is with you wherever you go."
>JOSHUA 1:8–9 NLT

Understand:

* How is God specifically calling you to be strong and courageous right now?

* Are you thriving at meditating on God's Word day and night, or do you need to improve on this?

* So far in your life, how has God given you success for your obedience to Him?

Apply:

God had called Joshua to be the one who would lead His people into the Promised Land after wandering in the desert for forty years under Moses' leadership. And in Joshua 1, you can read the powerful pep talk God gave to Joshua to help him be the brave new leader. It's not just for Joshua though. This scripture is a powerful pep talk from God to you as well, in whatever situation you find yourself. You have the whole Bible, the complete Word of God, including accounts of the life, teachings, death, and resurrection of Jesus Christ, plus the many books that came after the Gospels, to study, memorize, and meditate on. And you have the gift of the Holy Spirit living in you to instruct and guide you as well. So, just as He did for Joshua, God will lead you in the wonderful purposes He has for your life as you follow His Word with strength and confident courage.

Pray:

Heavenly Father, thank You for guiding me through Your Word. Please help me to focus on it day and night and live a life of obedience to it. I believe that only then will I truly prosper and succeed. Thank You for being with me wherever I go. Amen.

HE PICKS YOU UP

Read PSALM 40

Key Verse:

> *He lifted me out of the pit of despair, out of the mud and the mire. He set my feet on solid ground and steadied me as I walked along.*
> PSALM 40:2 NLT

Understand:

- ✳ How has God lifted you up in the past?

- ✳ Has God ever used another person to pick you up, set you on solid ground, and steady you as you walked along? How did you realize God was using that person?

Apply:

Nobody—not even the most self-sufficient among us—can go through life alone. We each have our own struggles, temptations, pitfalls, and burdens that weigh us down and threaten to pull us into what Psalm 40:2 calls a "pit of despair."

Because our Savior, Jesus Christ, stepped out of heaven and lived on earth, He experienced all these same issues. And He is faithful to lift us up out of any muddy pit of sin and shame we may find ourselves in.

There are any number of ways He rescues us. From the encouragement and intervention of a friend or a new sense of hope given to us by the Holy Spirit to a new perspective on a problem or a new purpose and peace that passes understanding—in a matter of a moment, the Father God can set you on solid ground.

If you're in a pit—no matter how deep it is—cry out to God. No hole is your ultimate destination. He will hear you and is faithful to answer. Soon you'll find yourself safely in His arms.

Pray:

God, thank You for rescuing me. For pulling me out,
cleaning me up, and giving me the confidence to walk ahead.
Stay with me, and keep me from stumbling or jumping
headfirst into another pit of my own making. Amen.

BLESSED ARE THOSE WHO HAVE NOT SEEN

Read JOHN 20:19–29

Key Verse:

> *Jesus said to him, "Have you believed because you have seen me? Blessed are those who have not seen and yet have believed."*
>
> JOHN 20:29 ESV

Understand:

* Are you a "I won't believe it until I see it" person?

* Why do you suppose Jesus said that those who have not seen are more blessed?

Apply:

Near the end of the Gospels, we find a remarkable story about one of the disciples—Thomas. The world knows him as "Doubting Thomas," but Jesus might disagree with that assessment.

Here's the backstory: Jesus had died on the cross just a few days prior. Thomas saw it with his own eyes. He knew that his friend, his mentor, his teacher, was gone. There was no disputing that cold, hard fact.

Now the other disciples were talking crazy, saying stuff like, "We've seen Him!" Had they lost their minds? Thomas, always the pragmatist, wanted proof. "Unless I see in his hands the mark of the nails, and place my finger into the mark of the nails, and place my hand into his side, I will never believe" (John 20:25 ESV).

The Lord made him wait for the proof. Eight days later, Jesus showed up, laying to rest any concerns that Thomas might have had. In an instant, as he touched the wounds in Jesus' hands and side, all doubts disappeared. The doubter became a believer.

Pray:

> *Lord, help me in my unbelief. There are so many times*
> *I want proof. I want to see things with my own eyes.*
> *I know that I will be more blessed if I can learn to trust*
> *You, even when I can't see. Help me, I pray. Amen.*

BUILT ON AND ROOTED IN JESUS

Read MATTHEW 7:24–27; LUKE 6:47–49;
JEREMIAH 17:7–8; COLOSSIANS 2:6–10

Key Verses:

> Just as you accepted Christ Jesus as your Lord, you
> must continue to follow him. Let your roots grow
> down into him, and let your lives be built on him.
> Then your faith will grow strong in the truth you were
> taught, and you will overflow with thankfulness.
> COLOSSIANS 2:6–7 NLT

Understand:

* How do these four different scripture passages relate?

* In what active ways do you continue to strengthen your
  foundation and grow your roots deeper into Christ?

Apply:

If we're in the middle of a storm but have a solid structure
in which to take refuge, we still have a strong sense of peace.
But if we're caught in a tent in the middle of an open field
when tornadoes pop up or we're in a shack on the sandy
beach of a raging sea, anxiety prevails. And we sure don't

build a trustworthy tree house in a tree without strong roots. So, if it seems anxiety is prevailing too much in our lives, maybe we need to reevaluate and reinspect our shelters and foundations. Have we built on something solid that will last or on things that are weak and temporary? Are there any damages or cracks? Are we continuing to check and repair and strengthen our foundations if needed? Are we nourishing and growing strong roots? Everything of this world is shaky and fleeting, and only what is built strong on and rooted deeply in Jesus Christ and the truth of His Word will endure.

Pray:

Loving Savior, please help me to constantly keep fortifying my foundation on You and growing my roots deeper into You. Show me the cracks and weaknesses, and help me repair and strengthen them. Please keep my faith strong and unwavering, no matter the storms of life. Amen.

CHALLENGE YOURSELF

Read PHILIPPIANS 3:7–21

Key Verses:

> I do not say that I have received this or have already become perfect. But I keep going on to make that life my own as Christ Jesus made me His own. . . . My eyes are on the crown. I want to win the race and get the crown of God's call from heaven through Christ Jesus.
>
> PHILIPPIANS 3:12, 14 NLV

Understand:

* What are you willing to sacrifice in order to become more like Jesus Christ?

* How can you push yourself in your faith to complete the race where the finish line is heaven?

Apply:

If anyone should've been satisfied with the state of his faith, it was the apostle Paul. This giant of the early church experienced a miraculous conversion (see Acts 9), after which he became a world missionary. He wrote nearly half of the New Testament and endured persecution and prosecution for the sake of sharing Jesus Christ. And yet, he knew he still had more growth to do, pressing himself closer to Jesus.

When you accepted Jesus into your life, it wasn't the end of the journey. Whether we've been a Christian for decades or are new to faith, each of us has space to advance toward our ultimate goal of eternal life with the Father, Son, and Holy Spirit in heaven.

What are you doing today to run the race? Sprinting, jogging, or walking, we're each at our own pace. Keep going and do not give up!

Pray:

God, I am ready for this challenge. This is a race that fills me with joy, and I want to run with excellence. Pick me up when I stumble, and set me on solid footing so I will run again. Amen.

TEMPTATION

Read GENESIS 3

Key Verse:

Now the serpent was more crafty than any of the wild animals the LORD God had made. He said to the woman, "Did God really say, 'You must not eat from any tree in the garden'?"
GENESIS 3:1 NIV

Understand:

* Have you ever tried to rationalize a sin that you know you are committing against God?

* What will you do the next time Satan tempts you to disobey God?

Apply:

Satan appears as a serpent in Genesis 3. He tempts the first people, as he tempts believers today, in a sneaky manner.

Adam and Eve had heard God clearly. He had given them free rein in the garden. They could eat of any tree *except* one. He had not restricted them in a harsh way. They had great freedom. They were given one rule, one tree to avoid, one guideline to obey.

Satan was crafty in his approach, wasn't he? He uses this technique with believers today as well. Use caution if you begin to think to yourself: *Does God really have such a guideline for my life? Would He really limit me in this way? Is this really a sin? Is it really so bad?*

God's standards and His rules are for our good. He has drawn boundary lines for us in pleasant places (see Psalm 16:6). Don't let Satan tempt you to believe otherwise.

Pray:

God, I am sorry for rationalizing sin. I try to find a way to make sin okay, but sin is never to be swept under the rug. Help me to walk in Your ways and to recognize sin as sin. Please give me strength to withstand temptation. In Jesus' name I pray. Amen.

CHOOSE EXTRAORDINARY

Read ROMANS 12

Key Verse:

> *Do not conform to the pattern of this world, but be transformed by the renewing of your mind.*
> ROMANS 12:2 NIV

Understand:

* What is one thing or who is one person you would describe as "extraordinary"? What makes this thing or person extraordinary?

* God created you for an extraordinary purpose. Think of one passion He has put in your heart. How can He use that today for great things?

Apply:

Wake up; be awesome. Oh, if only it were that easy! But the messages the world shouts keep us feeling inadequate. We're not good enough, beautiful enough, smart enough, thin enough, or rich enough. Soon these messages take root in our hearts, and we're telling ourselves these same lies. Satan knows the ins and outs of that game.

But those lies don't have to be the words you focus on today. This morning, choose to make this day extraordinary by living out God's plan for your life. Romans 12 gives guidance on how to do just that. Refuse to listen to the world's lies, and instead focus on the renewal that God promises. Focus on the talents God has given you, and use them today—for His glory. Intentionally show God's love to those around you today.

Your loving heavenly Father created you for more than a mediocre existence. Choose this day and every day to live an extraordinary life in Christ.

Pray:

Father, I admit most days I feel more ordinary than extraordinary. But You call me to greatness, not because of what I can achieve, but because of Your holiness and Your unending love for me. Each day I aspire to be more like You: more extraordinary than the day before. Amen.

REBUKE THE WAVES

Read MARK 4:35–41

Key Verse:

> *He got up and spoke sharp words to the wind. He said to the sea, "Be quiet! Be still." At once the wind stopped blowing. There were no more waves.*
> MARK 4:39 NLV

Understand:

* Life presents unexpected storms sometimes. Think of one that caught you off guard. How did Jesus calm the storm?

* What role can you play as a storm calmer in the lives of others?

Apply:

Jesus wasn't bothered by the storm. In fact, He was sound asleep below deck. The disciples, however, were in a panic, convinced they were going down. To still their beating hearts, Jesus rose and spoke a few sharp words to the wind and waves: "Be quiet! Be still." Immediately the storm ceased.

Likely, you've been through a few storms in your life. The

death of a loved one. A tough illness. A bad diagnosis. A job loss. Relationship troubles. Storms have a variety of faces. But they often throw us into a state of panic, much like the disciples found themselves in that night.

We have to remember that Jesus is in the boat with us. No matter what we're walking through, He's right there. And with just a word, He can calm the storm. "Anxieties, be still!"

Job situations can turn around. Sick bodies can be mended. Broken relationships can be restored. Lives can be changed in an instant if we just take our hand off the rudder and turn things over to the Lord.

Pray:

> *Lord, I'm so glad You're the storm calmer!*
> *You've intervened in my life so many times I've*
> *lost count. Thank You for staying with me in*
> *the boat. I'm so grateful, Lord. Amen.*

EXPERIENCE GOD'S PEACE

Read PHILIPPIANS 4

Key Verses:

> Don't worry about anything; instead, pray about
> everything. Tell God what you need, and thank him for
> all he has done. Then you will experience God's peace,
> which exceeds anything we can understand. His peace will
> guard your hearts and minds as you live in Christ Jesus.
> PHILIPPIANS 4:6–7 NLT

Understand:

* Do you have any disagreements with other women, like
  Euodia and Syntyche did, in your life right now that you
  need to resolve and reconcile?

* Do you do well in thinking about things that are true,
  honorable, right, pure, lovely, admirable, excellent, and
  worthy of praise? How can you be constantly growing
  and improving in this (verse 8)?

Apply:

God's Word promises that if we pray rather than worry about
everything, telling God what we need and thanking Him

for what He has done, then we will experience God's peace beyond all our understanding. It doesn't say God will instantly fix our problems or immediately give us whatever we ask for, but it promises inexplicable peace, the kind only God can give. Talking to God in prayer with gratitude demonstrates our trust in Him and love for Him. It reminds us of all He has done and is able to do. It fills us with confidence that He has sovereign power over all things, including every detail of our lives. We draw closer in relationship with our Father the more we talk to Him in prayer. The closer we are to the Father, the more we realize we need less of anything else and simply more of focusing on Him, who He is, and all He is able to do, to be in perfect peace.

Pray:

Heavenly Father, remind me that every problem pales when I focus on You. I thank You for all You have done, and I trust You to provide all that I truly need. Please fill me with Your extraordinary peace. Amen.

149

LET PEACE REIGN!

Read MATTHEW 26:17–30

Key Verses:

> While they were eating, Jesus took bread, and when he
> had given thanks, he broke it and gave it to his disciples,
> saying, "Take and eat; this is my body." Then he took a cup,
> and when he had given thanks, he gave it to them, saying,
> "Drink from it, all of you. This is my blood of the covenant,
> which is poured out for many for the forgiveness of sins."
> MATTHEW 26:26–28 NIV

Understand:

* The disciples didn't have a full understanding of what
  was coming, but they chose to spend as much time with
  Jesus as possible. Have you done that in your own life?

* What does the word *communion* mean to you?

Apply:

Have you ever thought about what was going through the
hearts and minds of the disciples on the night they broke
bread with Jesus? Did they realize that He only had a few
more hours with them? Did they understand that He would

actually pass away and then rise again?

Surely the disciples had the same attitude that we so often have today—they were hoping for the best but psychologically preparing for the worst. (How many times have you done that?)

Sometimes we have an inkling that something rough is coming; other times we're caught off guard, completely unaware of what's around the bend. We do a lot of things to guard our hearts, to avoid anxiety. But God wants us to know that, even in the darkest valleys, He's still in control. He's still right there, whispering, "Peace, be still." So go on. . .drink from the cup. Break the bread. Commune with Him. For only in spending time with Him will true peace be found.

Pray:

Father, when I take the time to commune with You, to really spend time in Your presence, it makes such a difference in my attitude. Today I choose the peace that comes from being with You, Lord. Amen.

I NEED HUMILITY

Read JAMES 4:6–10

Key Verse:

> *"God is opposed to the proud,*
> *but gives grace to the humble."*
> JAMES 4:6 NASB

Understand:

* What does the word *grace* convey to you?

* How do you think pride might act as a wall between you and God?

* Notice the effect of pride in your life. What feels good about pride? What aspects of pride have turned hurtful for you?

Apply:

There's a healthy kind of pride, a sense of God-given dignity that is the birthright of each of us—but that's not the sort of pride that this scripture is talking about. The word translated as "proud" was a Greek word that meant, literally, to think of oneself as better than others. *Humble*, on the other hand, meant someone willing to take a lower position. HELPS

Word-Studies defines scriptural humility as "being God-reliant rather than self-reliant." When we rely on God rather than ourselves, we have humility.

Selfish, egotistical pride can form a hard shell around our hearts. Sometimes it takes the tears of genuine sorrow to wash it away. Then when we finally come into God's presence, naked, low, with no more pretense, He will lift us up.

Pray:

> *God, my proud heart needs Your grace. Wash me with humble tears. I want to come closer to You. Amen.*

A CHEERFUL GIVER

Read 2 CORINTHIANS 9

Key Verse:

> So let each one give as he purposes in his heart,
> not grudgingly or of necessity; for God loves a cheerful giver.
> 2 CORINTHIANS 9:7 NKJV

Understand:

* When you give, do you do so cheerfully or begrudgingly?

* Where do you think your attitude toward giving originated? Does it need any modification or fine-tuning after reading this passage?

Apply:

Have you read the picture book called *The Giving Tree* by Shel Silverstein? It's about a tree that gives and gives to a young boy. As the boy grows, his needs change. The tree willingly gives shade and its branches to the boy. The boy grows old, and the tree has become just a stump, having given tirelessly and completely. The tree meets his final need by providing a place for the old man to sit and rest awhile.

As the reader, it's tempting to grow angry with the boy. But in the end, we see that the tree was happy to give to the boy all his life. It found joy in giving.

Are you like the boy or the tree? Are you a taker? Or are you a giver? When you give, do you give with a joyful attitude? Or do you give so that you might be noticed or praised for your act?

Pray:

Heavenly Father, I ask that You reveal to me any change that needs to take place in my heart regarding giving. Whether it is my time, my talents, or my money, I pray that I will give with an open heart and open hands. Make me a cheerful giver, I ask in Jesus' name. Amen.

TAKE DELIGHT IN THE LORD

Read PSALM 37:1–9

Key Verse:

> *Take delight in the LORD, and he will*
> *give you the desires of your heart.*
> PSALM 37:4 NIV

Understand:

* What does taking delight in the Lord mean to you?

* In what ways do you imagine the Lord delights in you?

* Is Psalm 37:4 saying that God will give us *anything* we ask for? Why or why not?

Apply:

Children are experts in delight. Watch a one-year-old gleefully play with the box her birthday present came wrapped in, and you are witnessing true joy. We can learn much from her today.

Our outlook determines how we interact with the world around us. When we're thankful for and take joy in simple pleasures, disappointments and frustrations become minor bumps in the day rather than catastrophes that derail us.

When we count our blessings instead of focusing on what we don't have, we realize how well God provides for us. When we delight in the Lord and praise Him for His goodness and His perfect plan for us, we live safely in the center of His will—the very best place to be.

How is God delighting you today? Spend time this morning looking for ways to be joyful. Whether He's doing big things in your life right now or you simply reflect on His unending faithfulness, live each day as an expert in delight.

Pray:

Lord, You fill me with such joy. Today my heart is singing as I delight in You. You are a good, good Father who gives me care, compassion, and kindness every day. Because of You, I have everything I need. Let my heart draw close to Yours, Father. I praise You because of who You are. Amen.

WHERE WILL YOU BE AT THE END OF TODAY?

Read PHILIPPIANS 3:7–21

Key Verses:

> *I focus on this one thing: Forgetting the past and looking forward to what lies ahead, I press on to reach the end of the race and receive the heavenly prize for which God, through Christ Jesus, is calling us.*
> PHILIPPIANS 3:13–14 NLT

Understand:

* What can you realistically accomplish today?

* What goals are worthwhile to pursue today? Are there others that aren't worth the time?

* What do you need to forget to allow you to move forward to the future?

Apply:

What's the state of your to-do list? Whether it's a mile long or blessedly under control, life is busy. Stay up late or get up early, we each have only twenty-four hours a day to get everything done.

There are tasks and responsibilities we must attend to,

but the apostle Paul, writing to the Philippian church, challenges us to focus on the bigger picture—to make it our priority to know Jesus and experience the mighty power that raised Him from the dead.

How can you come closer to that goal today? You're starting out the day right by spending time in His Word and in prayer. Lean on Him throughout the day, and ask Him to guide your steps, your thoughts, your words, and your actions. Commit to seeking Him every morning, taking a step (or a leap) closer to the glory of your Brother, Jesus.

Pray:

Jesus, I'm forgetting about my past when I struggled to know my true goals from day to day. Now I'm running toward You. Give me the wisdom to continue in that race while I pursue daily responsibilities. I know when I am doing both, my life can and will glorify You! Amen.

A TIME FOR EVERYTHING

Read ECCLESIASTES 3

Key Verse:

> To everything there is a season, a time
> for every purpose under heaven.
> ECCLESIASTES 3:1 NKJV

Understand:

* Which of the verses in Ecclesiastes 3 have you experienced (e.g., a time to mourn)? Are there any that you have not yet experienced?

* What does it mean that God is sovereign? How is His sovereignty seen in this chapter?

Apply:

Have you experienced some of the times mentioned in Ecclesiastes 3?

When a child dies, there is a time to mourn. There is also a time to be silent—simply out of an understanding that there are no words for such a loss. That is the time to be there for the family but not the time to try to fix it with words. The less spoken, the better.

There is a time to rejoice. Have you rejoiced at baptisms, weddings, and other special events? Certainly, these call for celebration.

There are times to weep and times to laugh. Thank God that sorrow comes in waves. Just as the mighty ocean tosses us a strong breaker and we lose our balance, there comes a period of calm when we maintain our footing once again.

Accept the sovereignty of God. Accept the changes that life will throw your way. There is a time for everything.

Pray:

Heavenly Father, help me to know how to react to change in my life. Guide me as I seek to find the balance between laughter and sorrow, rejoicing and mourning. Life is an adventure. Thank You for being with me in every time and in every season. Amen.

HE ALWAYS KNEW YOU

Read JEREMIAH 1

Key Verse:

> "Before I formed you in the womb I knew you,
> before you were born I set you apart; I appointed
> you as a prophet to the nations."
>
> JEREMIAH 1:5 NIV

Understand:

* If God knew you before you were born, He must have carefully selected the location and year of your birth as well. What if you had been born a hundred years sooner?

* God set you apart to do great things. What does that mean to you? What great things do you hope to accomplish?

Apply:

As you ponder the story of Jeremiah, as you think about how God called him into ministry, think of your own life. Consider the notion that the Creator of the universe knew you before you were born. He was there all along, carefully choosing your parents, your place of birth, even the year you would enter the world.

When you take the time to truly analyze these things, it's easy to see how special you are to God. He cared enough about you, even before birth, to plot out your entrance to the planet. He could have chosen any time, any place, but He knew just when to drop you onto the scene so that you could have the greatest impact for the kingdom of God. Wow!

God is at work, even now. Can you feel the anticipation stirring in your heart? He's got amazing things for you. Sure, there will still be a few bumps and bruises along the way. The road ahead will be filled with twists and turns, but He will guide you (and use you) every step of the way. So, lay down those anxieties and take His hand. He's got this!

Pray:

Father, thank You for arranging the details of my life.
It amazes me to think that You chose my parents,
my lineage, my hair color, my personality, and so on.
I'm also tickled to think that You chose for me to be
born in the very year I was born and in the very location
I was born. Wow, Lord! You've covered it all. Amen.

I WANT TO HAVE MY OWN WAY!

Read 1 PETER 4:1–8

Key Verse:

> *Since Jesus went through everything you're going through and more, learn to think like him. Think of your sufferings as a weaning from that old sinful habit of always expecting to get your own way.*
> 1 PETER 4:1 MSG

Understand:

* In what areas of your life is it hardest for you to give up your own way?

* When you don't get your way, does it cause you pain? How might this pain be put to spiritual use, allowing you to become more like Jesus?

Apply:

From the time we were babies, we've been crying and frustrated every time we couldn't get our own way. As we've grown older, we may have learned to disguise this better. We may have figured out other ways aside from yelling and having a tantrum to get what we want, but we still really want what we want!

Even Jesus struggled with this. That's why He prayed in the garden, sweating drops of blood as He begged His Father to find another path for Him to take, one that didn't lead to the cross. And yet, regardless of His natural longing to escape suffering and death, again and again He placed the entire situation back in His Father's hands. "Not My will," He said, "but only Yours."

Do we have the courage to follow His example?

Pray:

> *Free me, Jesus, from the tyranny of my selfishness.*
> *Wean me from the babyish habit of wanting my own*
> *way. Keep me wide awake and alert to the Spirit,*
> *as You were when You prayed in the garden. Amen.*

TRUE REPENTANCE

Read JOEL 2

Key Verse:

Rend your heart and not your garments. Return to the LORD
your God, for he is gracious and compassionate, slow to anger
and abounding in love, and he relents from sending calamity.
JOEL 2:13 NIV

Understand:

* Have you ever truly felt brokenhearted over your
  own sin?

* In Joel 2:13, what adjectives are used to describe God's
  reaction to one who returns to Him? In other words,
  to one who repents of sin.

Apply:

How easy it is for us to stand in judgment of the Israelites as
we read the stories of how quickly they forgot God's blessings.
But we do the same, do we not?

When you sin, God is watching your reaction to that sin.
He knows you will fall. We are living in a fallen world. But
do you try to hide your sin? Do you diminish it, thinking to

yourself, *Well, compared to this other person, I am not much of a sinner at all?*

Sin should break our hearts. God desires to see more than an outward expression of this brokenness. At the time of Joel, the people tore their clothing to express sorrow over sin. True repentance involves an inner sorrow, a tearing of the heart. God is quick to forgive when we come before Him broken and sorry for our sin.

Pray:

God, examine my heart. Show me if there is any attitude about my sin that displeases You. If I am quick to dismiss it as "not so bad," humble me. Remind me that You are holy and that sin is sin. Break my heart over my sin that I might truly repent and know Your gracious compassion in my life. Amen.

WHEN ALL GOES WELL

Read MATTHEW 21:1–11

Key Verses:

Most of the crowd spread their cloaks on the road, and others cut branches from the trees and spread them on the road. And the crowds that went before him and that followed him were shouting, "Hosanna to the Son of David! Blessed is he who comes in the name of the Lord! Hosanna in the highest!"
MATTHEW 21:8–9 ESV

Understand:

* It's ironic to think that Jesus was ushered into Jerusalem with such fanfare, only to be crucified shortly thereafter. What do you think He went through emotionally?

* Have you ever walked through a season of favor that was quickly followed by a season of loss?

Apply:

What an amazing day this must have been! Jesus entered Jerusalem, riding on a colt, to a welcoming crowd—one filled with onlookers and fans who cried out, "Hosanna to the Son of David! Blessed is he who comes in the name of the Lord!" They spoke blessings over Him, words of affirmation and adoration.

What different words they shouted a week later, as Jesus carried the cross to Golgotha. On that day onlookers jeered, spit on Him, and ridiculed Him.

A lot can change in a week.

Maybe you know what it feels like to be favored one moment then disregarded and cast aside the next. Maybe your husband left you for another woman. Maybe your child stopped speaking to you. Maybe you were overlooked by your boss, passed over for a promotion.

When all goes well, it's easy to shout words of praise. But when things are crumbling around you, depression and anxiety can set in. Today God wants you to know that He's got your back, no matter what you're going through. Good or bad, happy or sad, He will get you through this.

Pray:

I needed that reminder, Lord! I don't want to celebrate only when things are going my way. I want to be found faithful, even during the hard seasons. May I never forget that You won't let me go, Father. Amen.

BECAUSE YOU ARE WITH ME

Read PSALMS 23–25

Key Verses:

The Lord is my Shepherd. I will have everything I need. He lets me rest in fields of green grass. He leads me beside the quiet waters. He makes me strong again. He leads me in the way of living right with Himself which brings honor to His name. Yes, even if I walk through the valley of the shadow of death, I will not be afraid of anything, because You are with me.

PSALM 23:1–4 NLV

Understand:

* When have you felt you've truly been in the valley of the shadow of death? How did you feel God's presence with you there?

* Do you feel hated by anyone like David clearly did in Psalm 25:19? How does this passage help give you peace about that situation?

Apply:

One of the most familiar and popular passages of scripture is Psalm 23. Its comfort and peace abound as we picture God caring for us like a good shepherd lovingly cares for his sheep. God never leaves us as He guides, protects, and provides for us, until one day we are safely home with Him forever in heaven. Psalm 24 goes on to praise God for His greatness, glory, and holiness, acknowledging that everything in the world is His. And Psalm 25 pleads with God for direction, protection, and forgiveness of sin, trusting that He gives it and is full of goodness to those who love and obey Him. As you end each day, the praise and prayer in the psalms are beautiful ways to turn your heart and mind to God, letting Him give you the peace you need to rest well and prepare for a new day full of His plans, provision, and mercy.

Pray:

Heavenly Father, You are my loving shepherd, and I want to follow Your leading in all things. Please gently prod me back where I belong when I stray from Your good paths and plans for me. Forgive me for my sin and help me to obey You. Amen.

KEEP GOING

Read GALATIANS 6:1–10

Key Verse:

> Do not let yourselves get tired of doing good. If we do not
> give up, we will get what is coming to us at the right time.
> GALATIANS 6:9 NLV

Understand:

* How do you persevere when you feel as though your efforts for God's kingdom are in vain?

* How can you know you're spending time on the things God wants you to be doing for Him?

* How can you rest without stopping?

Apply:

Oftentimes doing good work in the Lord's name is its own reward. Although we aren't saved by our good deeds, when we're demonstrating God's love to others through our efforts, we're helping to further His plan on earth. What could be better?

But other times and in some seasons of life, doing good work may feel like a burden. We may be overextended or putting unrealistic expectations on ourselves and others. The work and our attitude about the work may even be straining relationships with family and friends. Even while doing God's work, it's possible to feel far from Him.

Still, the apostle Paul says, don't give up doing good.

If you're feeling tired of doing good, look at the big picture. Ask God to renew your passion for His work and to show you what He wants you to do. Pause to rest when necessary—not disengaging entirely but allowing yourself to recharge. God will reward your faithfulness!

Pray:

God, when life gets crazy, I start to develop a bad attitude about the good things You have given me to do. Renew in me a passion for Your work. Give me eyes to see how my efforts play a part in Your plan. And encourage me in my work so I can stay excited and vitalized to do it. Amen.

WATER INTO WINE

Read JOHN 2:1–12

Key Verse:

> "A host always serves the best wine first," he said. "Then, when everyone has had a lot to drink, he brings out the less expensive wine. But you have kept the best until now!"
>
> JOHN 2:10 NLT

Understand:

* Why do you suppose the line about the best wine being served first matters in this story?

* Have you ever wondered why Jesus chose to perform His first public miracle at a wedding?

Apply:

All the Gospels give us insight into the life of Jesus, starting with His childhood and moving into His ministry years. At thirty years of age, Jesus found Himself at a wedding. The host ran out of wine (a cultural no-no). Jesus' mother came to Him to ask a favor: "Son, do You think You could. . ."

Jesus' first response was to tell her that the time had not come. Then, after thinking it through, He performed His very first miracle—turning water into wine.

There's a lot of debate about why His first miracle took place at a wedding and why He chose turning water into wine. Some would argue that a miraculous healing (restoring sight to the blind, causing deaf ears to hear) might have been more impressive.

But Jesus chose to perform an "everyday" miracle, one that shows us He cares about the little things—when the faucet is leaking, when the car breaks down, when the refrigerator stops working. You can cry out to Him, even in the everyday things, and He's ready with a miracle. What a loving Savior we have.

Pray:

> I'm glad You care about the details, Lord. I can go
> to You with every concern, every problem. If You
> took the time to bless a wedding host and his guests,
> I know You will meet my every need. Amen.

GIVE YOUR BURDENS TO THE LORD

Read PSALMS 55–56

Key Verses:

When I am afraid, I will put my trust in you. I praise God for what he has promised. I trust in God, so why should I be afraid?

PSALM 56:3–4 NLT

Understand:

* What causes you to panic sometimes? How has God shown you He sees and cares?

* Have you ever been totally betrayed by someone you were once close to? What did God teach you through that experience?

Apply:

David's panicky words in Psalm 55:4–6 (NLT) are sometimes oddly comforting in a misery-loves-company kind of way. He says, "My heart pounds in my chest. The terror of death assaults me. Fear and trembling overwhelm me, and I can't stop shaking. Oh, that I had wings like a dove; then I would fly away and rest!" We feel awful for David, yet if we've experienced any kind of horrible upset, we can probably relate. And it's good to know we're not the only ones who've ever felt that way—terrified with a racing heart and wishing we could just fly away quickly to find peace and rest. Like David, we can vent our feelings of total fear and frustration to God. We can tell our heavenly Father about our panic and pain. No one understands and cares like He does. As we cry out, we must hold on to the promise that our good Father sees every one of our sorrows. If we trust in Him, He will guide us to and send us the help we need. He rescues us, defends us against our enemies, and helps us walk confidently in His life-giving light.

Pray:

Heavenly Father, I relate to David in his panic sometimes.
Please calm me with the truth of Your promises. Please
send me the help and encouragement I need. Please
guide and direct me through Your people, provision,
and perfect peace. I trust You, and I love You! Amen.

SPEAK GENTLY

Read PROVERBS 15

Key Verse:

> *A gentle answer turns away wrath,*
> *but a harsh word stirs up anger.*
> PROVERBS 15:1 NIV

Understand:

* In your experience, how has a gentle response defused a tense situation?

* In what situations or relationships are you more likely to respond with a harsh word?

* Do you think you'd ever regret using gentleness in an exchange?

Apply:

Words are powerful. Cliché? Yes, but that doesn't make it any less true.

Thoughtless words can unintentionally wreck someone's day. Careless words can lead to confusion and misunderstanding. Intentionally hurtful words can create lasting damage. And words used as weapons to slash at others can take a tense exchange and escalate it to a full-on angry battle.

But thoughtful, gentle words have the opposite effect and can be just as mighty. Words spoken in kindness can *make* someone's day. Encouraging words can start to rebuild a battered self-image. Loving words can mend bridges and tear down walls of resentment. A gentle response can lead to peace.

Today and every day, choose your words carefully. Thoughtfully consider the way you speak to your family, friends, frenemies, coworkers, and even yourself. Ask God to fill your heart, mind, and tongue with wisdom to speak gentleness.

Pray:

> *God, I need help controlling the words that come out of my mouth. You know the people and the situations that light me up and make me see red. But I have a choice in my reactions and responses. I want to choose gentleness. I want to bring Your peace into every situation. Show me how, because I can't do it by myself. Amen.*

DON'T LET YOUR HEART BE TROUBLED

Read JOHN 14:1–27

Key Verse:

> *"I am leaving you with a gift—peace of mind and heart. And the peace I give is a gift the world cannot give. So don't be troubled or afraid."*
>
> JOHN 14:27 NLT

Understand:

* How does the promise of Jesus preparing a place for you in heaven help keep your heart from being troubled here on earth?

* Do you relate to Thomas, Philip, or Judas in this passage? Why?

Apply:

Some of Jesus' disciples were clearly confused here in this passage. That's kind of comforting, isn't it? These men had spent so much time with Jesus. They had sat under His teaching. They had seen Him perform miracles. Time and again He had proven for them that He is God, and yet they still doubted and questioned! That ought to give you comfort and peace when you are doubting and questioning too. Thomas, Philip, and Judas had spent time with Jesus in the flesh. Here we are, thousands of years past when our Savior lived and taught in person on the earth, and yet we hold on dearly to our faith in Him. So, if Jesus patiently, lovingly, answered *their* questions, surely He has even more patience and love for *ours*. Maybe some nights you are praying questions like Thomas, Philip, and Judas asked. In those times, remember the answers Jesus gave: He is the way, the truth, and the life. He is God. He reveals Himself to those who seek after Him, obey Him, and love Him. He has sent the Holy Spirit to live in us and help us and remind us of everything He taught. And He offers peace that is out-of-this-world awesome!

Pray:

> Dear Jesus, thank You for Your patience and love for those who question and doubt like I do sometimes. Through Your Holy Spirit who is in me, remind me of all You have taught and promised. Please lead me and guide me in Your Word, reveal Yourself to me, and fill me with Your extraordinary peace. Amen.

ALIVE!

Read MARK 16

Key Verses:

> As they entered the tomb, they saw a young man dressed
> in a white robe sitting on the right side, and they were
> alarmed. "Don't be alarmed," he said. "You are looking
> for Jesus the Nazarene, who was crucified. He has risen!
> He is not here. See the place where they laid him."
>
> MARK 16:5–6 NIV

Understand:

* The resurrection of Jesus is one of history's most
  compelling events. What does it mean to you?

* Why would the resurrection of Jesus cause alarm?

Apply:

If you've ever attended a funeral or visited a grave site, the last
thing you expect is for the body to go missing. But that's what
happened in this, the most famous death scene ever written.
Jesus died on the cross and was buried in the tomb, but on the
third day, He sprang back to life.

The entire gospel story hinges on this one event: the

resurrection. If Jesus hadn't risen from the grave, if His death on the cross had ended the story, would we still be celebrating Him today? The resurrection seals the deal! It shows us, His followers, that death has no hold on us. We're meant to live forever with Him. It's also proof positive that Jesus was who He said He was, the Savior of mankind. For only a Savior would rise again with power and authority. And that same authority has been given to us, His kids.

What graveclothes are holding you back today? Speak with authority over your situation and watch as resurrection power springs you from death to life.

Pray:

> *Thank You for the resurrection, Lord! You are exactly who You claimed to be—Messiah and King. Thank You for the authority You've given me. I want to live with resurrection power, no matter what I'm going through. Death has no victory over me. Amen!*

HE IS ALWAYS KIND

Read TITUS 3:3–8

Key Verses:

> When God our Savior revealed his kindness and love,
> he saved us, not because of the righteous things we had
> done, but because of his mercy. He washed away our sins,
> giving us a new birth and new life through the Holy Spirit.
>
> TITUS 3:4–5 NLT

Understand:

* How have you tried to earn God's favor?

* Why is trying to earn God's favor a futile endeavor?

Apply:

Of all the characteristics of God, His kindness toward us is one that we should praise Him for every day. Kindness seems like such a simple thing, but it goes hand in hand with His passionate love for His children. His kindness allows us to approach Him when we know we've messed up. His care for us helps us to be confident that He will not condemn us in our sin when we sincerely repent and ask for forgiveness. His kindness was what resulted in His plan for our salvation through Jesus Christ.

We can't earn His kindness. He cannot be kinder to us or love us more if we say the right things or act a certain way. He loves us so much that He offers us new life in the Holy Spirit.

Your kind Father is waiting to hear from you. What is on your heart today that you'd like to tell Him? He will not judge you. He will respond in love. . .and in kindness.

Pray:

Father, when I think of all the ways You demonstrate how You love me, I realize just how kind You are to me. You bless me in so many ways, and You give me an identity in Christ that is perfect and whole—not dependent on my own goodness or abilities. Give me opportunities to show Your kindness to others today. Amen.

LIVE IN THE LIGHT

Read 1 JOHN 1–2

Key Verse:

>*But if we live in the light, as God is in the light,*
>*we can share fellowship with each other. Then the*
>*blood of Jesus, God's Son, cleanses us from every sin.*
>1 JOHN 1:7 NCV

Understand:

* What is the opposite of light?

* What do you think it means to live in the light versus to live in the darkness?

Apply:

As Christians, we have found the light, but the world around us still dwells in darkness. Darkness comes in many forms, but it is always the opposite of God's best. God is light. He exposes darkness with light.

Those who are spiritually blind walk in darkness. They are on a sinful path. If they had the light, they would turn and take another path—the path that leads to heaven. But as it is, they are on the path to hell.

At times, you may feel as if you are in the dark. Depression may overtake you. You may feel that God has left you. He hasn't. It is at those times that you must rely on the truth of scripture. God has promised to never leave you. He has rescued you from sin and set you on a path of righteousness. Remember in the darkness what you know to be true in the light.

Pray:

Lord, help me always to walk in the light as You are in the light. Keep my heart and mind pure even as I live in the midst of an evil culture that promotes sin. Father, when I feel that I am in the dark, remind me that I am a child of the light. I know You, and I am forever saved from sin and destruction. In the powerful name of Christ I pray. Amen.

GOD IS IN YOUR CORNER

Read HEBREWS 13:6–19

Key Verse:

> So we say with confidence, "The Lord is my helper;
> I will not be afraid. What can mere mortals do to me?"
> HEBREWS 13:6 NIV

Understand:

* Can trust in God and fear exist at the same time? Why or why not?

* When anxiety starts to creep in, what can you do to remember that God is on your side?

Apply:

Confidence is such an attractive quality, isn't it? Whether it's someone who can easily command the attention of the room or speaks in public flawlessly or simply excels at their job, it's inspiring and motivating to see someone who has it all figured out. Spoiler alert: the truth is that most of the time, even confident people have real fears.

Real, lasting confidence isn't something that comes from within us and our abilities. And confidence that truly conquers fear is rooted in the fact that, as Christians, we have God on our side. He is fighting for us, protecting us, and making us strong in spirit, heart, and mind.

Where in your life do you need an extra dose of confidence? The Lord is your helper. All you need to do is ask for His guidance and His help. With Him in your corner, you can overcome anything!

Pray:

Father, I need Your help. I trust You, but fear keeps trying to force its way into my heart and mind. I can't shake these feelings of uncertainty. My brain keeps fretting over scenarios that I know will probably never happen, but I can't stop the thoughts by myself. Fill me with Your peace. Give me the confidence that You are in control and You want the best for me. Amen.

HE'S GOT YOU COVERED

Read RUTH 3

Key Verses:

"Wash, put on perfume, and get dressed in your best clothes. Then go down to the threshing floor, but don't let him know you are there until he has finished eating and drinking. When he lies down, note the place where he is lying. Then go and uncover his feet and lie down. He will tell you what to do."

RUTH 3:3–4 NIV

Understand:

* Through good times and bad, God's got you covered. Think of a time when He proved this to you.

* Has anxiety ever left you feeling vulnerable? How did God cover or protect you during this vulnerable season?

Apply:

The story of Ruth and Boaz is one that brings great hope to those who feel lost and alone. Precious Ruth lost her husband at a young age. Her mother-in-law, Naomi, slipped into the role of mentor and friend. The two became so close that Ruth clung to the older woman, even returning to Naomi's homeland with her after the family tragedy.

When push came to shove in Ruth's life, she continued to look to Naomi for advice. Through Naomi, she eventually found her husband-to-be, Boaz, a man who swept her into his fold and covered her with the edge of his robe.

Do you have a Naomi or Boaz in your life? Who covers you, shields you when you're vulnerable? Have you become that person for others? Perhaps there's a friend, mentor, family member, or coworker who shares her thoughts with you. Or maybe you've become a Naomi to a younger woman in your world.

This special bond between younger woman and older is so precious. God wants all His girls—regardless of age—to learn from one another and to grow in the faith as their friendships grow as well.

Pray:

Lord, thank You for placing godly women in my life—women I can learn from, bounce ideas off of, and share personal concerns with. It's difficult to be anxious with so many friends cheering me on. I'm so grateful for them, Lord. Amen.

GOD SEES THE HEART

Read 1 SAMUEL 16

Key Verse:

But the LORD said to Samuel, "Do not look at his appearance or at his physical stature, because I have refused him. For the LORD does not see as man sees; for man looks at the outward appearance, but the LORD looks at the heart."

1 SAMUEL 16:7 NKJV

Understand:

* What are some common methods that we as humans use for judging others? (For example, by social class, by level of education, by race. . .)

* According to 1 Samuel 16:7, how does the Lord judge a person?

Apply:

Young man after young man paraded before Samuel. Their father, Jesse, probably watched Samuel expectantly. Don't you imagine he looked for a sparkle in Samuel's eye or a nod of his head to indicate the son who would be chosen to serve as king? And yet, Samuel said again and again, "This is not the one the Lord has chosen."

Jesse couldn't imagine that the chosen one could be the youngest, David, who was tending the sheep.

When young David stood before Samuel, the Lord pronounced him the chosen one. David was anointed with oil, and the Spirit of the Lord came upon him.

How do you see those around you? Or even yourself? Do you judge by the outward appearance or by the heart? God sees the heart.

Pray:

Help me, Lord, not to judge a book by its cover. While a person may do or say all the right things, it is their heart that You see. The race, social status, and even personality of a person is not what You see. You see the heart. Help me to follow Your example in this. Amen.

A NEW YOU

Read 2 Corinthians 5:11–21

Key Verse:

> *Therefore, if anyone is in Christ, he is a new creation.*
> *The old has passed away; behold, the new has come.*
> 2 Corinthians 5:17 esv

Understand:

* In what ways do you try to change yourself for the better? Physically? Mentally? Emotionally? Spiritually?

* Many fairy tales deal with transformation (Cinderella, the Little Mermaid). Why do these stories resonate with us at any age?

Apply:

There's something thrilling about an extreme transformation. From a professional makeover to a weight loss in the triple digits, we cheer for the individuals in these stories as they seek to change themselves for the better. To gain more confidence. To get healthier. Their improved selves are revealed, and they often are empowered by the change.

These kinds of physical changes are well and good, but they aren't eternal. Only God can truly transform us into new creations, perfectly forgiven because of the sacrifice of Jesus on the cross. Our old, sinful selves *die*. We are no longer who or what we were, and God's great mystery of new creation happens. We're not a better version of ourselves; we are made *new*. And whole. And perfectly loved.

Have you grasped fully the fact that you are new, sister? You aren't used, washed up, or a secondhand treasure. Your new self is *here*, now. Today, celebrate your newness in Christ!

Pray:

Thank You, Lord, for making me new. You did not leave me in my own sinfulness, and You have such abundant life for me to live out as Your loved child. I want to live each day in eager anticipation of new experiences with You. Draw me close, Father. Continue to make me more like You. I long for continued transformation! Amen.

CONSOLATION

Read JEREMIAH 31

Key Verses:

> *The Lord appeared to us in the past, saying: "I have loved you with an everlasting love; I have drawn you with unfailing kindness. I will build you up again, and you, Virgin Israel, will be rebuilt. Again you will take up your timbrels and go out to dance with the joyful."*
>
> JEREMIAH 31:3–4 NIV

Understand:

* Have you ever walked through a season where you felt inconsolable? How did you get through it?

* How has God used you to console a friend or loved one?

Apply:

Jeremiah is known as the weeping prophet. Maybe you can relate to that description. Perhaps you're the sort of person who feels things deeply, who has a hard time hiding your emotions.

The truth is Jeremiah had a lot to weep over. He faced persecution from those who disagreed with him, conflicts with false prophets, and untold plots against him.

Perhaps you've felt like that at times, like the whole world is conspiring against you. Maybe you've adopted a "What's the point?" attitude. Things are just too hard. The pressure is too great. Your anxieties have gotten the best of you.

If so, then look up! Your redemption is drawing near. Jeremiah's story ended triumphantly, with God's assurance that He would turn mourning into dancing. He will do the same in your life. No matter what you're going through right now, redemption is coming. God will rebuild, restore, and renew your life and give you purpose once more.

Pray:

Thank You for restoring my life, Lord. I don't want to live in defeat. I want to lift my eyes, dry my tears, and give every anxiety to You. I know I can trust You, Father. Amen.

GOD'S ECONOMY

Read PSALMS 113–114

Key Verses:

> *He raises the poor from the dust and lifts the*
> *needy from the ash heap, to make them sit*
> *with princes, with the princes of His people.*
> PSALM 113:7–8 NASB

Understand:

* How did Jesus humble Himself when He came to earth? Why did He do this?

* God often chooses the lowly over those with wealth or power. Name some examples of this from the Bible.

Apply:

In this world, often those with power or money appear to end up on top. They drive the fancy cars, have the best jobs, and experience all the luxuries this life has to offer. In God's economy, things are quite different. He often chooses to exalt the humble.

God chose a prostitute named Rahab to provide protection for some of His men. He even sent His own Son to earth to be born in a manger and to be raised in the home of Joseph, a carpenter. Jesus called fishermen as His closest disciples, those who "did life" with Him throughout His earthly ministry!

Praise God today for being God. There is no other like Him, as Psalm 113 declares. Thank Him for seeing the hearts of men and women rather than just the exterior. Remember to see others as God sees them. They are precious in His sight regardless of their status or state.

Pray:

> Lord, You are able to turn things around in our lives. Psalm 113 states that You give barren women children. You seat the poor at Your table as guests. Thank You for loving us so. Amen.

LET THE LORD REFRESH YOU

Read Isaiah 58

Key Verse:

> The Lord will always lead you. He will meet the needs
> of your soul in the dry times and give strength to
> your body. You will be like a garden that has enough
> water, like a well of water that never dries up.
> Isaiah 58:11 NLV

Understand:

* What makes your soul feel dry at times? How do you let
  God refresh you?

* How do you apply verses 13–14 in your life?

Apply:

Do you have plants in your home that are near death because
no one remembers to water them? They start to look pretty
sad, don't they? Or think of your lawn or garden in the middle
of a hot summer with no rain. Sometimes we start to feel
dry and ugly like that in our souls when we aren't spending
good time with God. We need to read His Word and pray and
worship Him so that He can lead and refresh us. We also need

to fellowship with other believers who regularly do these things. God gives the kind of living water that makes us never feel thirsty again. When Jesus spoke to the woman at the well, He meant it for us too: "Whoever drinks the water I give them will never thirst. Indeed, the water I give them will become in them a spring of water welling up to eternal life" (John 4:14 NIV).

Pray:

> *Lord, please lead me. Meet the needs of my*
> *soul in dry times, and give strength to my soul.*
> *Thank You for refreshing me and restoring me*
> *with Your extraordinary living water! Amen.*

GOD'S GOOD CREATION

Read PSALM 19:1–6

Key Verse:

> *The heavens are telling of the greatness*
> *of God and the great open spaces above*
> *show the work of His hands.*
> PSALM 19:1 NLV

Understand:

* When has God's creation awed you so much that you couldn't help but worship?

* What does God's creation reveal to you about His character? His aesthetic preferences?

* What one thing do you think is most interesting or fascinating in all of God's creation?

Apply:

Our God delights in transformation. From the caterpillar changing to the butterfly to the seasonal cycles of the leaves of deciduous trees, creation constantly changes according to His masterful plan. The sky—what Psalm 19 refers to as "the heavens"—may be the best example of constant change.

Consider how the sunrise's Creator uses different palettes of color and varying brushstrokes each day to fill the sky with beauty. And the night sky is no different as God directs the moon's phases and lights up the vast expanse with innumerable pieces of light.

The heavens say so much about God's greatness without using a single word.

Today, really look at God's creation. Raise your eyes to the sky. Kneel to be eye level with a child. Notice a flower or a bird's song or a dog's bark. He created our world— including you—for His pleasure and for our blessing.

Pray:

Creator God, today I am celebrating Your artistry throughout all of Your creation. Even in nature around me every day, I can learn much about You. Give me Your eyes to appreciate and delight in the things You delight in. I praise You for the master artist You are. You have made all things good and pleasing in Your sight. Amen.

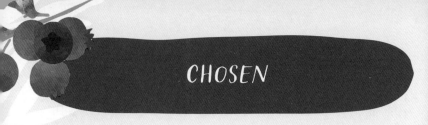

CHOSEN

Read 2 KINGS 2:1–22

Key Verse:

> *As they were walking and talking, a chariot and horses*
> *of fire appeared and separated Elijah from Elisha.*
> *Then Elijah went up to heaven in a whirlwind.*
> 2 KINGS 2:11 NCV

Understand:

* How did Elijah go to heaven?
* Who had remained very close to Elijah until he was taken up into heaven?

Apply:

Elisha had refused to leave Elijah until the very end. He had stuck to him like glue, a faithful friend. Perhaps he wanted to see Elijah taken up into heaven in order to confirm and strengthen his own faith. Perhaps he just wanted to be with him as long as he possibly could. What we do know is that he remained faithful. He refused to leave Elijah's side.

When Elijah asked Elisha what he could do for him, the only desire Elisha expressed was to have a double portion of his spirit. He didn't want wealth or fame, only to be very well equipped to serve God.

Do you stand by and support your spiritual mentors, those who are teaching and preaching the gospel as Elisha supported Elijah? Do you stick closer than a brother? And what is your desire in doing so? Do you desire to learn as much as you can and to serve God in an even greater way?

Consider your loyalty and your motives. You will be blessed if they are pure before God.

Pray:

Lord, I do not understand the mystery as to why Elijah was lifted into heaven as he was. Make me as faithful as Elisha to the work of Your kingdom. Help me not to desire any other thing than more of Your Spirit, greater ability to serve and love You better. Amen.

PERFECT TIMING

Read JOHN 11:1–44

Key Verses:

When Mary reached the place where Jesus was and saw him, she fell at his feet and said, "Lord, if you had been here, my brother would not have died." When Jesus saw her weeping, and the Jews who had come along with her also weeping, he was deeply moved in spirit and troubled. "Where have you laid him?" he asked. "Come and see, Lord," they replied. Jesus wept. Then the Jews said, "See how he loved him!"
JOHN 11:32–36 NIV

Understand:

* When have you felt that God failed to show up or was too late to help you?

* Have you heard it said that God's timing is perfect? What evidence from scripture gives this statement validity?

Apply:

Mary and Martha grieved the recent loss of their beloved brother, Lazarus.

The sisters, known from Luke's Gospel to be different in nature, had one thing in common here. They knew if Jesus had been there sooner, Lazarus would not have died.

This statement, which both Mary and Martha make in the passage, reveals much. They had faith that Jesus could heal. They knew He was the only hope. And neither saw how this story could have a happy ending. Their brother was dead.

Jesus was not late to the scene. The Messiah did not check His watch, realizing too much time had passed. Jesus, as always, was right on time.

A greater miracle than healing took place that day in Bethany. Lazarus rose from the grave after being dead for four days. He came forth at the sound of the Master's voice. And that day, the angels in heaven surely rejoiced because many believed.

Pray:

Jesus, when it seems You are taking too long, remind me that Your timing is perfect. You are never too early or too late. You are always right on time. Grant me faith in the waiting and in the times I cannot understand Your ways. Amen.

HE THINKS OF YOU

Read MATTHEW 10:24–31

Key Verses:

> "Are not two small birds sold for a very small piece of
> money? And yet not one of the birds falls to the earth
> without your Father knowing it. God knows how many
> hairs you have on your head. So do not be afraid. You
> are more important than many small birds."
> MATTHEW 10:29–31 NLV

Understand:

* If you've ever been forgotten or overlooked, how can
  it change your perspective to know that God thinks
  about you?

* How does it make you feel that God knows you so well
  that He has the hairs on your head numbered?

Apply:

Our God is not some far-off, cosmic force who created us
and then sat back to watch us implode. Even in the middle of
our own self-implosion (sin), God is there, loving us back to
Himself so we can be in a right relationship with Him.

Maybe today you're feeling forgotten by friends or family. Rejected, overlooked, unloved. When other humans fail us, God is steadfast in His care. He celebrates with us in our victories and comforts us in our tragedies. He rejoices when we make good choices and lovingly disciplines us back to the right path in our failures. We are on His mind and constantly in His heart.

Today, relax in His constant care. Thank Him for knowing you and loving you so perfectly. You are priceless to Him.

Pray:

Father, sometimes I feel overlooked, unloved, and forgotten by others. I try not to dwell on it, but it hurts me deeply. Help me to remember that I am always in Your thoughts. You love me with a fierce love. When it comes down to it, God, You are all I need. Amen.

WALK IN WISDOM

Read 1 KINGS 3:16–28

Key Verse:

> Solomon said, "Don't kill the baby." Then he
> pointed to the first woman, "She is his
> real mother. Give the baby to her."
> 1 KINGS 3:27 CEV

Understand:

* Solomon was quick on his feet! He came up with the
  perfect solution to the problem, didn't he? Can you
  think of a time when you were quick on your feet?

* Where do you need the most wisdom—at home, work,
  or school, or with your relationships?

Apply:

Perhaps you've heard someone say, "You have the wisdom of
Solomon." Maybe you've wondered what that meant. What
gave Solomon the edge wasn't just his wisdom but his ability
to discern a situation and then make decisions based on his
discernment.

Two women showed up with one baby, each arguing that

the baby belonged to her. How would Solomon solve the problem? In a very interesting way! He instructed them to cut the baby in half. Of course, the real mother cried out in anguish while the wannabe mom agreed to Solomon's terms. It was obvious in a flash who the real mom was.

Maybe you want the wisdom of Solomon. It's easy to acquire. The Bible tells us that we're all able to tap into that well. But while you're at it, also ask the Lord for discernment. Wisdom and discernment work hand in hand, after all.

Pray:

Lord, thank You for discernment and wisdom.
I can't drum these things up on my own,
but You freely give them to me when I ask.
Today, I ask. Fill my cup, Lord. Amen.

YOU ARE YOUR FATHER'S DAUGHTER

Read 1 JOHN 3:1–10

Key Verse:

> *See how very much our Father loves us, for he*
> *calls us his children, and that is what we are!*
> 1 JOHN 3:1 NLT

Understand:

* When you are getting to know someone, how do you explain and define yourself to them?

* In what ways do you struggle with your identity?

* How has your identity changed throughout your lifetime?

Apply:

Who are you? Mom, grandmother, daughter, granddaughter, niece, aunt, wife? Do you identify yourself as your occupation or a hobby or volunteer work or ministry?

All these things are good, and they do play a part in the way we interact with others, but none of these labels is lasting. Relationships, jobs, hobbies, volunteer opportunities, and even some ministries are part of our lives only for a season. In reality, our identity has nothing to do with what we *do*. Instead, our identity is grounded in the fact that we are handpicked daughters of God the Father. We are sisters to our risen Savior and King, Jesus Christ, and forever counted as forgiven, saved, and standing in the grace of God.

So, when life is in upheaval, when you're not sure who you are, instead remember *whose* you are.

Pray:

When my life, my roles, and my relationships are in flux, Father, remind me who I am. I am Yours. I am a daughter of the King. I am claimed by Jesus as a sister. I am a vital part of the body of Christ. I am forgiven, cherished, loved, and encouraged in You. Your identity is what I need. When people see me, let me fade into the background, and may Your light shine! Amen.

PRAYER AND PETITION

Read MATTHEW 6:9–13

Key Verse:

> *"This, then, is how you should pray: 'Our Father in heaven, hallowed be your name.'"*
> MATTHEW 6:9 NIV

Understand:

* Have you ever had to plead a case in court? What did it feel like, to speak before the judge?

* Isn't it wonderful to know you have instant access to the King of all kings, God Himself? What wows you the most about that idea?

Apply:

"Our Father in heaven, hallowed be your name." We know and love those words. They give us power and hope. They connect us to the King of the universe and remind us that He cares about even the smallest of details. Our ability to converse with our Creator, to offer our prayers and petitions, is such a privilege.

Many times, we come before the Lord with requests that seem overwhelming. A friend has a cancer diagnosis. A loved one has been in an accident. A friend's child has died. It's all too much to take in. But God wants us to bring those things to Him, to plead our case (no matter how difficult the need), and to release the burden to Him. For only in releasing the burden can we truly walk in freedom.

What are you holding on to today? What need feels too great? What burden is too heavy? What anxieties are too unnerving? Run to the Lord. Start with the words "Our Father in heaven," and go from there. He longs for you to bare your heart.

Pray:

Our Father in heaven. . .You are an awesome and amazing God! Thank You for Your willingness to listen to my pleas and move on my behalf. I'm so glad I can cast my cares on You, Lord. Amen.

THE WAY, THE TRUTH, AND THE LIFE

Read JOHN 14

Key Verse:

> *Jesus said to him, "I am the way, and the truth, and the life; no one comes to the Father but through Me."*
> JOHN 14:6 NASB

Understand:

* What three things does Jesus claim to be in this verse?

* What does it mean that no one "comes to the Father" except through Jesus?

Apply:

Throughout the Gospel of John, we find Jesus using the statement "I am" seven times. Jesus was bold to use this phrase because the name for God that meant "I Am" was so sacred to the Jews that they would not even utter it. Jesus claimed to be God because He is God. Jesus said, "I am the bread of life" (John 6:35 NASB). He also said, "I am the good shepherd" (John 10:11 NASB) and "I am the Light of the world" (John 8:12 NASB).

This powerful "I Am" statement in John 14:6 declares that

the only way to get to God is through Jesus. Other religions teach that good works will allow people to reach God. Some believe that God is in everything or that humans themselves are God. Christianity alone teaches that Jesus is the only way to the heavenly Father. Take comfort in the fact that you may come into the presence of God because you are a believer in the one who is the way, the truth, and the life: Jesus.

Pray:

Jesus, You are the way, the truth, and the life. I am so thankful to know You as my Savior. Thank You for dying on the cross for my sins, bearing them for me. Thank You for providing a way for me to spend eternity with God. Amen.

NEW CLOTHES

Read COLOSSIANS 3:1–14

Key Verse:

> *Therefore, as God's chosen people, holy and dearly loved, clothe yourselves with compassion, kindness, humility, gentleness and patience.*
> COLOSSIANS 3:12 NIV

Understand:

* When you experience God's compassion, how does that influence the compassion you show to others?

* Of the list of compassion, kindness, humility, gentleness, and patience, which is the easiest for you to demonstrate?

* Which is the most challenging for you to demonstrate?

Apply:

How much time do you take to choose an outfit each day? Do you lay it out the night before, complete with specific accessories? Or do you tug on whatever smells cleanest from the hamper?

Just as our physical clothes can say something about who

we are, Paul is urging his readers in Colossians 3 to clothe themselves with the attributes of Christ Jesus: compassion, kindness, humility, gentleness, and patience. Why does Paul use the clothing analogy? Because clothing is something that we must intentionally put on; we come out of the womb without wearing a stitch!

Which articles of Jesus' clothing does today call for? All these things layer well and help prepare you for any climate. Best of all, when you dress yourself in these clothes, you're looking even more like the love of God.

Today, take stock in the ways that God shows you compassion, kindness, gentleness, and patience. Ask Him for opportunities to show these to others as well.

Pray:

> God, I want to be more like You. You shower me with
> compassion and kindness. But my own selfishness
> gets in the way of being like You—I am proud and
> impatient with others. Help me to realize how much
> I have been forgiven, how much You love me, so that
> I can show this same love to others. Amen.

FOOD FOR DAYS

Read 1 Kings 17:7–16

Key Verse:

"For this is what the Lord, the God of Israel, says: 'The jar of flour will not be used up and the jug of oil will not run dry until the day the Lord sends rain on the land.'"

1 Kings 17:14 niv

Understand:

* Have you ever been through a season of lack, where provisions were in short supply? What did you do?

* How do you garner the faith to believe for the impossible during lean seasons?

Apply:

Imagine the plight of that poor widow woman. A child to feed. No way to replenish what little food she had in the house. And then, on top of everything, the man of God wants her to share? Must have felt impossible. And intrusive.

Now imagine how she must have felt, meal after meal, day after day, as the flour and oil replenished themselves. Surely she blinked, stared at her ingredients to make sure she wasn't losing her mind, and then blinked again. Wow!

Maybe you've been in her place. Your provisions were low. You wondered where the next meal was going to come from. From out of nowhere, a bag of groceries appeared on your doorstep. A gift card arrived from a friend. An unexpected check showed up in the mailbox.

God loves to replenish your storehouse, and His methods are always imaginative and fun. So don't fret. Don't be anxious about tomorrow. You won't go hungry. He's got this one covered.

Pray:

> *Thank You for Your provision, Lord. You've seen*
> *me through every lean season, making sure I had*
> *everything I needed and more. I'm so grateful. Amen.*

221

WE DO NOT LOSE HEART

Read 2 CORINTHIANS 4

Key Verses:

> *Therefore we do not lose heart. Though outwardly we are wasting away, yet inwardly we are being renewed day by day. For our light and momentary troubles are achieving for us an eternal glory that far outweighs them all.*
> 2 CORINTHIANS 4:16–17 NIV

Understand:

* What are the hardships weighing on you tonight? What do you need to cry out to God about them?

* How are you seeking God's power to keep you from losing heart and being defeated by your suffering? How are you being renewed day by day?

Apply:

Some days we feel exactly like verses 8 and 9 of this passage describe—hard pressed on every side, perplexed, persecuted, and struck down. Anyone who says the Christian life should be all good all the time clearly does not read their Bible entirely and in context! We should not run from or deny the hurts and hardships we experience. Feeling all the awful weight and pain of them and grieving them before God are what leads us to remember the powerful truth in that passage: Yes, we are hard pressed, *but we are not crushed*. Yes, we are perplexed, *but we are not in despair*. Yes, we are persecuted, *but we are not abandoned*. Yes, we are struck down, *but we are not destroyed*. How is that possible? Because God will never leave us or forsake us. He holds us up and strengthens us through the power of His Holy Spirit living in us. Jesus suffered and died for us, and we grow closer to Him as we share in suffering. At the same time, we show off His eternal life-giving power to others when we suffer but are never defeated—until one day in heaven when we learn the purposes of our hardships and we see the amazing rewards they were gaining us!

Pray:

Heavenly Father, please help me to see the value in these hardships I'm experiencing. They help me to know and to show off Your power and love as You strengthen and uphold me. I trust that they are achieving rewards for me so awesome that my mind cannot even imagine them. I am fully depending on You alone, Father, and I love You! Amen.

DO NOT GO ON SINNING

Read JUDE

Key Verse:

> I say this because some ungodly people have wormed
> their way into your churches, saying that God's marvelous
> grace allows us to live immoral lives. The condemnation
> of such people was recorded long ago, for they have
> denied our only Master and Lord, Jesus Christ.
>
> JUDE 1:4 NLT

Understand:

* Have you ever heard something that you instantly knew
  did not align with God's Word?

* What would you say to someone who said that because
  of God's grace we can live however we desire?

Apply:

The author of Jude urgently warns about ungodly people who
have "wormed their way" into the churches. He does not want
anyone to be led astray by them. These people said that due
to God's grace, it was fine to go on sinning. Sin was covered by
the grace of God anyway.

What a dangerous way to live! And what backward thinking! The apostle Paul taught in the book of Romans that our sinful lives were crucified with Christ and we were set free. Romans 6:18 (NLT) states, "Now you are free from your slavery to sin, and you have become slaves to righteous living."

Are there people in your life who claim to be Christians and yet live a sinful lifestyle? Just as the author of Jude warns the people of his day, be warned. It is often easy to be led astray by such people. You want to surround yourself with friends who point you toward godly living.

Pray:

Lord, please give me the discernment I need to distinguish the godly from the ungodly. I never want to be led astray by those who think of Your grace as a sort of insurance plan, assuring them of forgiveness no matter how they live. I want to honor You and live a godly life. In Jesus' name I pray. Amen.

WALK FAITHFULLY

Read GENESIS 6:1–9:17

Key Verses:

> *Noah found favor in the eyes of the* LORD. *This is the account of Noah and his family. Noah was a righteous man, blameless among the people of his time, and he walked faithfully with God.*
> GENESIS 6:8–9 NIV

Understand:

* What was most familiar to you about the story of Noah and the ark? What had you never heard of or thought much about before?

* What do Matthew 24:37–39 and 1 Peter 3:18–22 add to the story of Noah?

Apply:

Have you ever found yourself on a path that you're sure God led you to, but as you keep walking it, things start feeling really strange? You're afraid you've misunderstood what you were once certain was God's crystal clear direction. Noah must have felt that way too sometimes. He was righteous and blameless and walked faithfully with God, but you have to wonder if he started shaking his head in confusion at times when God gave instructions to build a giant boat, fill it with two of every animal on the earth, and then wait while rainwater flooded and destroyed the earth. Bewildered or not, Noah continued to obey God, and that took steadfast faithfulness and courage. In the end, God did exactly what He had said He would—He destroyed the earth with a great flood. Only Noah and his family and the animals they had gathered survived, safe inside the ark. Noah could be extremely grateful that he faithfully obeyed God whether he felt confused or not. If you find yourself trying to follow God's leading even when it doesn't make much sense, let Noah's story give you peace tonight. Let it remind you that with faithful, patient obedience, you will see God's hand and His rescue in His perfect timing.

Pray:

*Heavenly Father, please give me the peace and patience
I need to keep obeying You even when I don't fully
understand where You are leading and what You are doing.
No matter what, I want to trust and follow You! Amen.*

LIVE EVERY DAY IN AWE

Read PSALM 33:1–15

Key Verse:

> Let all the earth fear the LORD; let all the
> inhabitants of the world stand in awe of him!
> PSALM 33:8 ESV

Understand:

* When was the last time you were awestruck by God?

* Why is God worthy of our awe?

* Do you think it's possible to increase your awe of God in your everyday life? Why or why not?

Apply:

If you ever doubt the power of words, remember this: Our Creator God spoke the world into being (Psalm 33:9). "Let there be light," He said in Genesis 1:3 (ESV), and light appeared. From His infinite mind and artistic sensibility, He formed each mountain and star, each creature with its unique look and role in His plan. And then He sculpted us, the most beloved of His creation, intricate and beautiful living beings made in His own image.

He gave us free will and hearts geared toward relationship—with Him and with other humans. And He loved us with a love so great that He would sacrifice everything to allow us to be with Him after we messed up our perfect relationship with Him.

The whole earth is filled with awe-inspiring reminders of God's majesty. Today, pray and ask God to open your eyes to see the reminders as they truly are and stand in awe of Him.

Pray:

My Creator and King, show me the wonder of Your creation. In the life-giving nourishment of rainfall, in the majesty of a sunset, in the twinkling of points of light in the heavens, I am amazed. You provide everything I need, and what's more is You have made all things beautiful as well. Thank You, God. Amen.

DISCERNMENT THROUGH THE SPIRIT

Read 1 Corinthians 2

Key Verses:

This is what we speak, not in words taught us by human wisdom but in words taught by the Spirit, explaining spiritual realities with Spirit-taught words. The person without the Spirit does not accept the things that come from the Spirit of God but considers them foolishness, and cannot understand them because they are discerned only through the Spirit.

1 Corinthians 2:13–14 niv

Understand:

* Who is able to understand things that come from the Spirit of God? Who is not able to accept these things?

* What is the difference between these two types of people, and which type are you?

Apply:

The things of God seem foolish to those who do not have the Holy Spirit. When you accepted Christ, you were sealed with the Holy Spirit. This enables you to understand and apply God's Word and His ways.

Don't be surprised if unbelievers argue with you about the validity of scripture. They are wearing spiritual blinders. They are unable to see or comprehend scripture.

The Holy Spirit is our comforter and our counselor. The Holy Spirit enables us to understand and apply God's Word. Praise God that you do not wear a veil that keeps you from taking in His Word. Pray diligently for those you know who have not yet come to know Christ. Their lives depend upon the shedding of those spiritual blinders. They need the freedom that comes through the Spirit. They need Jesus.

Pray:

Heavenly Father, I thank You that I have the Holy Spirit. I am so thankful that I am able to understand Your Word and apply it to my life. It saddens me that so many see spiritual things as foolishness. I pray for repentance in their lives that they might accept Christ and receive the blessings of the Holy Spirit. Amen.

MIXED MESSAGES

Read GENESIS 11:1–9

Key Verse:

> *That is why it was called Babel—because there the LORD*
> *confused the language of the whole world. From there the*
> *LORD scattered them over the face of the whole earth.*
>
> GENESIS 11:9 NIV

Understand:

* The world sends so many mixed messages. Which ones confuse you the most?

* Why do you suppose God chose to confuse the language and scatter people across the face of the earth?

Apply:

Not long after Adam and Eve left the garden, an unusual event took place. The people (who had everything in common, including their language) began to build a tower to make a name for themselves. When God saw what they planned to accomplish, He chose to shake things up a bit. He confused their language and scattered the people.

Strange, right? God is usually all about unity, not division.

Why split up the people? Why scatter them across the globe? The truth is these folks were getting a little too puffed up. They were looking at themselves as heroes, saviors. Yes, they were working together, but only to bring glory to themselves.

Maybe you've been in a similar situation where a team effort ended up being about personal glory. Or maybe you've experienced excessive pride in a coworker or someone on a sports team. We can all get a little puffed up at times. As believers, we send a mixed message when we begin to tout ourselves instead of the Lord. It's time to refocus on Him, to take our eyes off ourselves so that He can be magnified.

Pray:

Father, I want to give all the glory to You. You're the only Savior I'll ever need. If I begin to sing my own praises, stop me, I pray. May I only live to praise You. Amen.

BUILDING YOUR HOME

Read PROVERBS 14

Key Verse:

> *The wise woman builds her house, but the*
> *foolish tears it down with her own hands.*
> PROVERBS 14:1 NASB

Understand:

* Proverbs 14 provides a contrast between two types of individuals. What are they?

* What are the verbs, or action words, in Proverbs 14:1? Consider the meaning of each. Which one do you spend most of your time doing?

Apply:

The home is a haven for a family. It's a place of peace where a family seeks refuge from the world. There are women who get this right and those who don't.

More often than not, the woman of the house sets the tone for the home. Are you setting a tone of peace or of strife? How do you greet your husband and children at the end of a long day? Do you instantly launch into a to-do list? Do you scold?

Or do you provide warmth, nurturing, and acceptance?

The wise woman seeks to meet the needs of her family. She is conscientious with finances. She encourages and builds up her husband and kids. She manages things rather than just letting them go. A home should not be a place of disorder and disarray.

Seek to honor God by being a builder rather than a destroyer of your home.

Pray:

Lord, forgive me for the times when I have forgotten the importance of my role. I want to be categorized as a wise woman and not as one who tears down her own home. Help me to be a student of my husband and children, learning them well, that I might know the ways I may build them up and encourage them best. Amen.

WATCHING OVER YOU

Read PSALM 71

Key Verses:

> For You are my hope, O Lord God. You are my trust
> since I was young. You have kept me safe from
> birth. It was You Who watched over me from the
> day I was born. My praise is always of You.
>
> PSALM 71:5–6 NLV

Understand:

* What are your earliest memories of being aware God
  was watching out for you?

* What times in your life has God seemed closest to you?
  Why?

* What times in your life has God seemed far away? Why?

Apply:

You've had lots of people in your life who have taken care of
you over the years—parents, grandparents, husband, siblings,
aunts and uncles and other relatives, friends, teachers,
coworkers, school staff, coaches, doctors, nurses, and on and
on. As an adult, you take care of yourself more, of course, but

you still need plenty of people in your life to call on for help with all kinds of things. Ultimately, though, God is the one who constantly watches over you. Praise and thank Him for His extraordinary care. It is God working through all of those who take care of you and help you when you need it. And He will for all of your life, like Psalm 23:6 (NLV) says: "For sure, You will give me goodness and loving-kindness all the days of my life. Then I will live with You in Your house forever."

Pray:

Heavenly Father, thank You so much for watching over me and guiding me through many people in my life. I trust that You will always provide the right people in the right places at exactly the right times when I need them. Amen.

ABOVE AND BEYOND

Read LUKE 5:1–11; JOHN 21:1–14

Key Verses:

> When He had finished speaking, He said to Simon, "Push
> out into the deep water. Let down your nets for some fish."
> Simon said to Him, "Teacher, we have worked all night and
> we have caught nothing. But because You told me to, I will
> let the net down." When they had done this, they caught so
> many fish, their net started to break. They called to their
> friends working in the other boat to come and help them. They
> came and both boats were so full of fish they began to sink.
>
> LUKE 5:4–7 NLV

Understand:

* What does Peter's first reaction to the miracle in Luke
  5:8 tell you about his character?

* In John 21:7, Peter jumped out of the boat and into the
  water as soon as he realized it was Jesus. Do you think
  you would have done the same? Why or why not?

Apply:

In Luke 5, at the very beginning of Jesus' earthly ministry, He
helped the fishermen catch far more than they could have

imagined. They had just spent the whole night fishing and had caught nothing, but Jesus only had to say the words and suddenly the fish were everywhere—enough to break their nets and sink their boat! And in John 21, we read how Jesus did a similar miracle, and this time it was part of how He was showing Himself alive again after His death and resurrection. Both times, the disciples must have been so amazed and overjoyed—and especially so after they had believed Jesus to be dead! Don't ever forget that God is able to provide so much more than you can possibly fathom—including eternal life! Keep trusting Him and asking Him for everything you need.

Pray:

Loving Savior, You go above and beyond to show how You love to provide. Thank You for meeting my day-to-day needs with plenty of extra blessing, and thank You especially for giving eternal life! Amen.

UNDERSTANDING OUR FREEDOM

Read 2 CORINTHIANS 3:7–18

Key Verses:

> *For the Lord is the Spirit, and wherever the Spirit of the Lord is, there is freedom. So all of us who have had that veil removed can see and reflect the glory of the Lord. And the Lord—who is the Spirit—makes us more and more like him as we are changed into his glorious image.*
> 2 CORINTHIANS 3:17–18 NLT

Understand:

* How does your life reflect the glory of the Lord?

* In what ways is the Spirit making you more like God?

Apply:

To really understand the freedom we have in Christ, we first must understand just how restrictive the old covenant was. Open your Bible to books like Leviticus, and you'll see lists of ceremonial, sacrificial, and moral laws. In order to be right with God, His people had to follow *each* of these laws. Break just one, and they were out of God's good favor. Living under the law was oppressive and exhausting, but the faithful also understood the effort was worth it—a blameless life meant fellowship with God—intimate friendship like Moses experienced on the mountain (see 2 Corinthians 3:13).

Under the new covenant of Christ, Jesus came to earth to satisfy all these laws and be the ultimate sacrifice for the sins of the world. No longer do we need to work to earn the Father's approval and to be His friend. All we must do is accept the free gift of grace that He offers. We don't have to climb a mountain to reflect the glory of God. We can experience His full life here, now, today!

Pray:

> *God, because of Jesus and the gift of Your Spirit,*
> *I know I live in freedom. Teach me how to live fully*
> *free and more like You each day. Amen.*

DO IT GOD'S WAY

Read GENESIS 16:1–15

Key Verse:

> *So after Abram had been living in Canaan ten years,*
> *Sarai his wife took her Egyptian slave Hagar and*
> *gave her to her husband to be his wife.*
> GENESIS 16:3 NIV

Understand:

* Sometimes, when our anxieties are high and our faith is low, we step out on our own and take matters into our own hands. Have you ever done that? How did it work out?

* Who was most to blame in this situation—Abraham, Sarah, or Hagar? Have you ever been in a situation where everyone involved got ahead of God?

Apply:

It doesn't take much effort to see that Sarah got ahead of God in this twisted tale. When she saw that she could not provide a child for her husband, she went to her maid and concocted a plan to keep Abraham's lineage going. Can you even imagine

Hagar's shock at Sarah's suggestion?

Now picture the jealousies that surely arose when Hagar's son, Ishmael, was born. Sarah, the very one who came up with the plan, was riddled with jealousy. If she had just waited, if she hadn't jumped the gun, she would have seen the fruition of God's plan in her own life. She should have waited on Isaac.

Maybe you know what it's like to get antsy, to feel like you need to come up with your own plan because God isn't moving fast enough to suit you. You let your fears and anxieties get the better of you. Anytime you do that, you're stepping out from under the umbrella of His protection and safety. It's better to hang on to your faith and believe that He will come through for you, even if circumstances make you feel otherwise.

Pray:

Lord, I don't want to get ahead of You! I don't want to take off down the road, thinking I've found a better way. Stop me in my tracks, I pray. Quiet my heart. May I stick close to You and trust in Your plan. Amen.

LIE DOWN AND SLEEP IN PEACE

Read PSALMS 3–4

Key Verses:

> Let the light of Your face shine on us, O Lord. You have
> filled my heart with more happiness than they have
> when there is much grain and wine. I will lie down and
> sleep in peace. O Lord, You alone keep me safe.
>
> PSALM 4:6–8 NLV

Understand:

* What causes you to shake with anger (Psalm 4:4)?
  Do you have any sin to confess because of that anger?
  How do you practice self-control to let God be the
  one to deliver justice?

* What does it mean to "look into your [heart] and be
  quiet" (Psalm 4:4 NLV)?

Apply:

The New Life Version of the Bible titles Psalm 3 a Morning
Prayer of Trust and Psalm 4 an Evening Prayer of Trust.
They timelessly give us courage today—if we meditate on
them and pray them day and night as well. No matter the

number or power of our enemies, they cannot compare to God's sovereign protection over our lives. No matter who is running after lies and spreading them like wildfire, God's truth prevails. No matter what is going on around us, we can lie down and sleep in peace because almighty God keeps us safe. We cry out to Him, and He hears our prayers. He shows us what is truly right and good.

Pray:

Heavenly Father, yes, please let the light of Your face shine on me. In a world full of evil and lies, I need to see Your goodness and remember Your truth every moment, day and night. Please lift my head when I am discouraged, and hear my prayers when I am crying out to You. I trust in You alone to give me rest and keep me safe. Amen.

GOD KNOWS YOUR FUTURE

Read JEREMIAH 29:1–23

Key Verse:

> "For I know the plans I have for you," says the
> LORD. "They are plans for good and not for
> disaster, to give you a future and a hope."
> JEREMIAH 29:11 NLT

Understand:

* When in the past did God work in a way that you did not expect?

* What do you fear about the future? Are your fears rational or irrational, and do you have any control over the outcome you fear?

Apply:

Whether we admit it or not, we all like to be in control. From deciding whether or not to buy a house to determining at what temperature to set the thermostat, there's nothing too big or too small that we'd like to have our say in.

What does the future hold? We may have plans and hopes and dreams, but the truth is we have little control over what happens today, tomorrow, or a decade from now. Left unchecked, our desire for control can cause sleepless nights or even strife in our relationships, and worry may spiral into despair.

But God, in His infinite wisdom and knowledge of all that has been and all that will be, cares about your future. Even when you are struggling with stress and uncertainty, God is working out your today for a hope-filled tomorrow. Live in His goodness, in His grace, and in His love.

Pray:

God, I give my future to You. Forgive me for acting as if I am in control, because I'm not. You're much better at it. I believe You have good plans for my today and my tomorrows. Align my desires with Your will so that I am living today and every day in You. Please be the Lord of my life, Father. Amen.

GOD WILL MAKE ALL THINGS RIGHT

Read 2 Samuel 7

Key Verse:

> *"Your house and your kingdom will endure forever before me; your throne will be established forever."*
> 2 Samuel 7:16 NIV

Understand:

* To whom does God reveal information about David in 2 Samuel 7?

* How does knowing that Jesus eventually comes from the line of David change the way you interpret God's promises to David in these verses?

Apply:

In the Garden of Eden, man made a choice to turn away from God. This is known as the Fall. Because of the Fall, we have death in the world. There was no physical death prior to it. We also have shame. Adam and Eve clothed themselves with fig leaves to hide from the Lord after they had sinned against Him. As a result of the Fall, things are not right in the world. Things are not as God designed and desired.

When God put King David on the throne, a promise was revealed. It was a promise that God was establishing a throne that would endure forever. How is that? Because Jesus Himself would come from the line of David.

Way back in 2 Samuel, God was working out a plan of restoration. Through Christ, we are reconciled with God. And one day, God will once again make all things right in His world. Heaven will be even grander than Eden!

Pray:

> *Heavenly Father, I thank You that on my darkest day and when I face my deepest disappointment, I can remember that You have overcome this world. You are working out Your plans just as You were in 2 Samuel. One day You will make all things right again. Amen.*

YOU ARE NEVER ALONE

Read JOHN 14:15–26

Key Verses:

"And I will ask the Father, and he will give you another Helper, to be with you forever, even the Spirit of truth, whom the world cannot receive, because it neither sees him nor knows him. You know him, for he dwells with you and will be in you."
JOHN 14:16–17 ESV

Understand:

* What does the Holy Spirit mean to you?

* Does the Spirit ever seem dormant inside you? Why do you think that is?

* What is one practical way you can engage with the Holy Spirit today?

Apply:

Jesus' disciples must've felt panicked. Their beloved Rabbi had said repeatedly He would soon leave them. And if He was sincere in His promise, what would they do without Him, the Son of God who guided them on the path of truth, answered their questions, challenged them, and comforted them?

They couldn't understand it then, but the helper that Jesus promised His Father would send would be so much more. Jesus came to earth to be God with us. The Spirit arrived to be God *in* us. Think of it! The same almighty, powerful God who spoke the world into existence has taken a home in your heart. . .forever!

You are not alone. You cannot be separated from God's love any more than you can be separated from His Spirit. Don't let this magnificent helper go unnoticed today! Breathe in the Spirit, and ask for help to live out God's plan today.

Pray:

Spirit of God, sometimes You are a mystery to me. But I long to know You better. Come alive in my heart today and make Your presence known. Jesus said You are my helper. So, I am asking for Your help. Help me even when I act like I don't need it. Amen.

GIFTED TO SERVE

Read 1 Corinthians 12

Key Verse:

> *Now to each one the manifestation of the*
> *Spirit is given for the common good.*
> 1 Corinthians 12:7 niv

Understand:

* When you look over the list of spiritual gifts, which ones stand out to you? Why?

* Is there an area of your life where you excel? What is your strongest gift, and how have you used it?

Apply:

If you've ever done a Bible study of the spiritual gifts, then it's likely you've taken a test to see which ones you possess.

Which gifts are your strongest? Are you called to minister through words of wisdom or knowledge? Do you have a prophetic gifting or the ability to pray for healing? There are so many ways to reach out to others using these gifts.

When you realize that God is the one working through you—that you don't have to figure it out on your own—then your anxieties are squashed. There's no need to fret. God's got this.

Open your heart to be used by God in the gifts of the Spirit; then watch as He touches others in a supernatural way . . .through you.

Pray:

Lord, how amazing! You've given me gifts to be used to reach others. Today I lay down my fears, my concerns, and choose to operate in those gifts, Lord. Use me, I pray. Amen.

GOD KNOWS WHAT YOU NEED

Read MATTHEW 6:25–34; LUKE 12:22–34

Key Verse:

> *"Look at the birds of the air; they do not sow or reap or store away in barns, and yet your heavenly Father feeds them. Are you not much more valuable than they?"*
> MATTHEW 6:26 NIV

Understand:

* What similarities and differences do you find in the two passages?

* What do you find yourself worrying about lately? How do these passages speak to those worries?

Apply:

What will we eat, what will we drink, what will we wear? Do you relate sometimes to the tone of that rather frantic series of questions? Maybe it's not literally food, beverage, and clothing that fill your mind with concerns right now, but the general idea could be the same. Most of our worries boil down to taking care of ourselves and our loved ones, both now and in the future. The higher our expectations and standard of living, the greater those worries might be because we'll have more to lose the more we expect and possess. So, we are wise to live as modestly as possible and hold gratefully and loosely to extra blessings beyond our most basic provisions. When we picture the refreshing simplicity of birds and flowers having beautiful purpose and being perfectly provided for, seemingly without a care in the world, we can be inspired to solely trust our Creator like they do. We are created in His image and are far more cherished and valued by Him. When we seek to know and love Him above everything else, we realize how everything we have is ultimately a gift from Him. He will never stop loving and caring and providing for us here on earth, and He is keeping all the very best gifts and treasures for us to enjoy perfectly forever in heaven.

Pray:

Heavenly Father, again and again I need to release my worries about my needs and the needs of my loved ones to You. No one sees and cares and provides as well as You do. Please help me remember to trust that. Thank You for all You have already provided for me. Help me to realize how so much of what I have is extra blessing on top, and help me to strive to be as generous to others as You are to me. Amen.

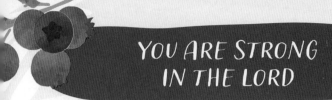

YOU ARE STRONG IN THE LORD

Read 2 CORINTHIANS 12:1–10

Key Verses:

> Each time he said, "My grace is all you need. My power works best in weakness." So now I am glad to boast about my weaknesses, so that the power of Christ can work through me. That's why I take pleasure in my weaknesses, and in the insults, hardships, persecutions, and troubles that I suffer for Christ. For when I am weak, then I am strong.
>
> 2 CORINTHIANS 12:9–10 NLT

Understand:

* Why does Paul admit to weakness in this passage?

* What challenges do you have that only God can overcome?

Apply:

The apostle Paul is a giant of our Christian faith. This man with a miraculous conversion story (see Acts 9) went on to preach the gospel, greatly encourage congregations to the ends of the earth, and pen thirteen of the books in the New Testament. By anyone's standards, Paul had much to boast about.

But here in 2 Corinthians 12, Paul downplays his accomplishments and instead focuses on his own weaknesses. We don't know what his specific difficulty was, but it was something that he could only overcome with God's help. And God's strength, Paul says, is best displayed through human weakness.

Where are your weaknesses, your struggles? Whether it's something physical, spiritual, mental, or emotional, turn it over to God. With the power of the Holy Spirit inside of you, His strength will be made perfect in your weakness.

Pray:

God, when this world tells me to be empowered by my own strength, remind me that I am nothing without You. It feels strange to say it, but I thank You for my weak spots. Fill those gaps with Your power, dear Lord, and I will be strong in You today and forever. Amen.

GOD GOES BEFORE YOU

Read DEUTERONOMY 31

Key Verse:

> "The LORD himself will go before you. He will
> be with you; he will not leave you or forget
> you. Don't be afraid and don't worry."
> DEUTERONOMY 31:8 NCV

Understand:

* What are the promises packed into the key verse
  for today?

* What challenge will you face less afraid knowing that
  the Lord goes before you?

Apply:

Regardless of the fact that God had promised them the land of
Canaan, the Israelites of the past had been too afraid to enter.
They feared the giants who lived in this amazing land. After
a period of forty years in the wilderness as God's punishment
for their lack of faith, this new generation was ready to go in.
It was critical that they hear the words of Moses or they too
might forfeit the land that flowed with milk and honey.

They were not to fear. God was with them. He would not leave them or forget them. They were commanded not to worry.

Where are you hesitant? Where do you need to step out in faith? When we shrink back from taking a step of faith where God is clearly leading us, we forfeit amazing blessings. Claim these promises in your own life today. God is with you. He goes before you. He will not leave or forget you. Trust Him.

Pray:

Heavenly Father, I will go where You lead. Help me to lay down fear and worry. I want to trade those hindrances in for Your help and Your faithfulness. I know that You go before me. Wherever You may lead, I will follow in faith. Amen.

A SECOND CHANCE

Read JONAH 1–3

Key Verses:

Then the LORD spoke to Jonah a second time: "Get up and go to the great city of Nineveh, and deliver the message I have given you." This time Jonah obeyed the LORD's command and went to Nineveh, a city so large that it took three days to see it all.
JONAH 3:1–3 NLT

Understand:

* Have you ever had a Jonah type of experience in your life?

* How have second chances from God helped you develop more faith and gratitude?

Apply:

Jonah is a great story to revisit when you feel like you've been called by God to a place or situation you don't really want to be in. Just like Jonah, you might be tempted to go in "the opposite direction to get away from the LORD" (Jonah 1:3 NLT). That's what Jonah did, and the consequences are an unforgettable lesson. None of us wants to end up in the belly of a whale, literally or figuratively, for disobeying God. But the best part of the lesson is remembering God's great love and gracious mercy toward us, evidenced especially in Jonah's prayer in chapter 2: "I cried out to the Lord in my great trouble, and he answered me. I called to you from the land of the dead, and Lord, you heard me!" (verse 2 NLT). Our holy God had every right to ignore Jonah for his disobedience, but instead He listened. He loved Jonah and had mercy on him, and you can feel Jonah's gratitude and praise in the words of his prayer. God gave Jonah a second chance, and the story reminds us that God loves to give us second chances as well.

Pray:

Heavenly Father, help me to remember Jonah when I'm feeling like I don't want to obey. Remind me of the lessons he learned. Thank You for Your grace and mercy to give me many second chances as well. Amen.

COUNT IT JOY

Read JAMES 1:2–18

Key Verses:

> Count it all joy. . .when you meet trials of various kinds,
> for you know that the testing of your faith produces
> steadfastness. And let steadfastness have its full effect,
> that you may be perfect and complete, lacking in nothing.
> JAMES 1:2–4 ESV

Understand:

* Does the promise of a stronger faith after enduring trials make it easier to endure them? Why or why not?

* What difficulties have you come through that resulted in a greater faith?

* How can you encourage someone who is going through a difficult time?

Apply:

It's easy to live a joyful life when the birds are singing, there's a spring in your step, and all is right with the world.

But this is real life, and if those carefree seasons come, they are woefully short lived.

James encourages us to count every difficulty, every bump in the road, and every dead end a joy. Why? Because challenges, frustrations, and disappointments grow our faith and dependence on God. He will strengthen you through anything life can throw at you and your family; and when you emerge on the other side, James says your faith will be greater, more perfect, and complete.

Are you in a difficult season now? Hold on, don't give up, and find joy in the fact that God is working. He will bring you through to a better tomorrow.

Pray:

Almighty Father, I long to experience Your joy. But it is hard to be joyful when everything is so difficult right now. Help me to look past the challenges of today to see what You're doing in my life and in my current situation. I love You and I trust You. Amen.

CAST THOSE CARES

Read JOHN 21:1–14

Key Verse:

> He said, "Throw your net on the right side of the boat and
> you will find some." When they did, they were unable to
> haul the net in because of the large number of fish.
>
> JOHN 21:6 NIV

Understand:

* Have you ever held on to your cares unnecessarily?
  When God asks you to toss them overboard, go for it!

* Can you think of a time when God told you to "fish" on
  the other side of the boat? He's in the provision business
  and wants to bless you.

Apply:

When Jesus instructed the disciples to cast their nets on
the opposite side of the boat, He was giving them several
opportunities at once: to obey, to trust, and to prosper. Maybe
He's given you similar challenges at times. He was also giving
them the option of doing things His way instead of their own.

It's not always easy to do things God's way, but when you

do, your burdens are lifted. As you cast that net on His side of the boat, you're releasing the cares and anxieties that came with trying to do things your own way.

What is God asking you to trust Him with today? Can you cast your net on His side of the boat, let go of your worries, and trust Him to give you a large haul? Get ready to obey, and you will see amazing results!

Pray:

Lord, today I choose to obey You—to toss my net on Your side of the boat that I might see a haul. I release my cares, my anxieties, and my need to control, and I choose to trust You instead. Praise You, Father! Amen.

265

HEAVEN IS MY HOME

Read PHILIPPIANS 3

Key Verses:

> But our citizenship is in heaven. And we eagerly
> await a Savior from there, the Lord Jesus Christ, who,
> by the power that enables him to bring everything
> under his control, will transform our lowly bodies
> so that they will be like his glorious body.
> PHILIPPIANS 3:20–21 NIV

Understand:

* What does it mean that your citizenship is in heaven?

* What will our bodies be like one day after the
  return of Jesus?

Apply:

Do you ever feel like you don't belong here? That's because
you don't! As Christ followers, we are aliens in this world.
We're just passing through. Our real home is heaven. So if
you feel out of place in the culture in which you are stuck, get
used to it. Though we are in the world, we are not of it. We are
bound for a greater place, and we will dwell there with new

bodies that are like that of our Savior.

While we don't know all there is to know of heaven, we know that our new bodies will be better than our current ones. We know there will be no more tears or death there. We know we will reign forever with our God.

When you don't fit in, it's okay. You are not meant to. Embrace it as homesickness. You are longing for paradise. One day you will feel right at home because you will be with your God in heaven.

Pray:

Lord, there are so many bad things on the news every night. People are hurting one another. This culture is upside down, calling sin okay and persecuting those who seek to be godly. Help me to recognize that I am in this world for a purpose but my real home is heaven. I look forward to the day I can be there with You. Amen.

THE MIGHTY VOICE
OF THE LORD

Read PSALMS 27–29

Key Verses:

> The voice of the LORD is over the waters;
> the God of glory thunders, the LORD thunders
> over the mighty waters. The voice of the LORD
> is powerful; the voice of the LORD is majestic.
>
> PSALM 29:3–4 NIV

Understand:

* How do these three psalms speak into your life and give you peace?

* In what concerns are you needing to clearly hear God's voice? Are you doing well in giving His voice the most attention?

Apply:

With so much social media and the entire internet carried around on our phones in our pockets and purses, we have constant, sometimes overwhelming, input into our lives from all kinds of sources, opinions, and persuasions. This can be a good thing when used wisely and a terrible thing without limits. It's easy to let far too many voices speak into our lives, especially when sometimes the loudest, worldly ones are the worst kind of influence. It can be a struggle to let God's voice be the one we give the most attention to. So, we have to constantly go to His Word, putting it above all other influence. Psalm 29 describes the great power of God's voice, and we can focus on this psalm as we ask God to speak more boldly and loudly into our minds and hearts than any other voice. He is our loving, guiding shepherd. We should constantly strive to know and listen to His voice and follow Him alone (John 10:27).

Pray:

Heavenly Father, please speak boldly and clearly to me. I want to hear Your voice above all others. Please help me to use wisdom and limits on how much I listen to other voices, and help me to give Yours top attention. Amen.

NO ONE ELSE LIKE JESUS

Read HEBREWS 7

Key Verses:

We need such a Religious Leader Who made the way for man to go to God. Jesus is holy and has no guilt. He has never sinned and is different from sinful men. He has the place of honor above the heavens. Christ is not like other religious leaders. They had to give gifts every day on the altar in worship for their own sins first and then for the sins of the people. Christ did not have to do that. He gave one gift on the altar and that gift was Himself. It was done once and it was for all time.
HEBREWS 7:26–27 NLV

Understand:

* Have you experienced opposition for your faith in Jesus? How does this passage help you handle opposition to your faith?

* How do verses 23–25 help give you great peace and gratitude?

Apply:

Throughout your life, people will challenge your faith in Jesus Christ and try to dissuade you, but belief in Jesus as God and the one and only Savior is the only religion that is right and true. We should share our faith peacefully and lovingly, never forcefully. Jesus alone was perfect and holy and without sin. He gave His own life once for all people of all time, and no other religion offers that kind of gift and love and miracle! To know Jesus as Savior is to simply believe in Him and accept the awesome gift He gave of grace and eternal life. He took our sins away when He died on the cross for them and then rose to life again. Hold fast to this awesome truth, and let God fill you with peace as you trust in Him.

Pray:

Loving Savior, thank You for giving Your life to save everyone who believes in You! There is no one else like You! You are God and You are Savior, and I am so grateful for You! Amen.

SIMPLICITY AND SINCERITY

Read 2 CORINTHIANS 1:12–24

Key Verse:

> For our boast is this, the testimony of our conscience,
> that we behaved in the world with simplicity and
> godly sincerity, not by earthly wisdom but by the
> grace of God, and supremely so toward you.
> 2 CORINTHIANS 1:12 ESV

Understand:

* Why do you think Paul is urging Christians to live with "simplicity and godly sincerity"?

* What pitfalls can come with living by "earthly wisdom"?

* In what ways can you simplify and live a more sincere life?

Apply:

It can be exhausting to try to keep up with current popular thought. From health and nutrition studies to politics and science, everything, it seems, is in a constant state of flux. It's impossible to know what the world sees as right and wrong, what's up and down, what's left and right.

While we should be aware of what's going on around us (we do live as nomads on earth, after all), Paul urges us not to get caught up in "earthly wisdom" but rather to live simply and with godly sincerity. What does this look like? When we follow Christ's commands—love God and love others—we are shining the light of the Father in a dark and confusing place. And reflecting a sincere heart in everything we do shows the world that we are focused and grounded in a life-giving faith. Living such a life will attract others to the saving grace of Christ!

Pray:

Jesus, I've tried for too long to live the way the world tells me I should. It's exhausting trying to have it all, understand it all, do it all, and look flawless in the process. Give me Your wisdom to know what is essential: love, generosity, truth, forgiveness. Help me to live a life of simplicity and sincerity rooted in You. Amen.

A RAINBOW OF PROMISE

Read GENESIS 9:1–17

Key Verse:

> *"I am putting my rainbow in the clouds as the sign
> of the agreement between me and the earth."*
> GENESIS 9:13 NCV

Understand:

* Have you ever reached the end of a long journey to find a rainbow of hope at the end?

* Why do you suppose God chose to use all the colors of the rainbow to signify hope?

Apply:

There are a variety of stories in the Old Testament where God made a covenant with man. Nearly every famous Bible character had some sort of encounter that would fall into this category. For Noah, however, the covenant was very unusual.

After the ark came to a halt on Mount Ararat, a rainbow filled the sky. Clearly, Noah, his wife, his sons, and his daughters-in-law had never seen anything like it. How they must have marveled at the arc of color shimmering in the sky above. Can you imagine the oohing and aahing?

God promised that He would never again destroy the earth with floodwaters, and He covenanted that promise by setting the rainbow in the sky.

Has God made any promises to you? How has He sealed those promises? Does He remind you in the middle of the storms so that you won't give up? He's not a promise breaker, after all.

Pray:

> *Father, I'm so glad You're a promise keeper!*
> *If You said it, I know You'll follow through. I'm*
> *grateful for the covenants You've made with me,*
> *Lord. You are worthy of my praise. Amen.*

GOOD MEDICINE

Read PROVERBS 17:13–28

Key Verse:

> *A joyful heart is good medicine, but a*
> *crushed spirit dries up the bones.*
> PROVERBS 17:22 ESV

Understand:

* Who or what can make you laugh no matter what?

* Whom can you be joyously silly with?

* What situation or friend needs an infusion of joy today?

Apply:

The writer of Proverbs tucked this little verse in the middle of a string of warnings—hard issues that life throws our way as well as pitfalls and types of people to avoid. From fights and foolish financial decisions to corruption and lying, it's a laundry list of pathways to ruin.

But, the writer seems to say, joy in the middle of all these things is good medicine—just what the doctor ordered.

Life is hard. Every day brings troubles—Jesus tells us so in Matthew 6:34—but how we choose to view and deal with those troubles is up to us. Look hard enough, and joy can be found in any situation. And viewed at the right angle and with a joyful heart, you may even find bright pockets of laughter in the darkest places.

Do you need an infusion of joy today? Look for the unique ways that God is shining light into your everyday life. And share that joy with others!

Pray:

Joyful Father, I am so thankful that You are a God who delights in laughter. You invite me to unburden my spirit (Psalm 55:22), and joy comes rushing in. Show me how to cultivate a heart bursting with Your hope and joy so I can share it with others. Give me pockets of laughter throughout my day. May it be Your soothing cure to my parched spirit and be a good medicine for everyone around me. Amen.

GOD WILL FIGHT FOR YOU

Read 1 SAMUEL 17

Key Verse:

> David asked the men standing near him, "What will be done for the man who kills this Philistine and removes this disgrace from Israel? Who is this uncircumcised Philistine that he should defy the armies of the living God?"
> 1 SAMUEL 17:26 NIV

Understand:

* Standing up to your enemies (especially the ones who loom over you) is tough! When was the last time you had to stand up to someone? How did the story end?

* Think of a time when God fought a battle for you.

Apply:

If you rewound the story of David and Goliath a bit, you would see a boy on his way to the battlefield with one purpose in mind: to deliver bread and cheese. David didn't head to the army's camp to fight. He was just a delivery boy. When he heard Goliath's taunts, though, everything changed. The delivery boy morphed into a warrior. With renewed vision, he reached for five smooth stones to take down his enemy.

Maybe you've walked a mile in David's shoes. You've somehow meandered into a situation, completely oblivious, never dreaming you'll soon be in the fight of your life. You're not even sure how you jumped from point A to point B, but there you are, standing before a giant. And you're scared. Anxious. Worried.

Isn't it wonderful to realize that God went ahead of young David and fought the battle for him? That's what He'll do for you too. Go ahead and reach for those stones. Equip yourself. But watch as the Lord of hosts fights this one for you.

Pray:

Thank You for fighting my battles, Lord! With Your help, I'll take down every giant who dares to rear his head against me! I'll praise You in advance for the victory. Amen.

FOR SUCH A TIME AS THIS

Read ESTHER 4

Key Verse:

> *"If you keep quiet at this time, someone else will help
> and save the Jewish people, but you and your father's
> family will all die. And who knows, you may have
> been chosen queen for just such a time as this."*
>
> ESTHER 4:14 NCV

Understand:

* How might God desire to use you in your current
  circumstances?

* Are you willing to take risks for the kingdom of God?

Apply:

The story of Esther reminds us of God's sovereignty. Through
a series of events, Esther, a Jewish orphan, became a queen of
Persia. When the time was right, God motioned Esther onto
the stage and used her in a starring role to save the Israelite
people.

God has orchestrated your life in a similar manner.
Consider the circumstances God has used in order to bring

you to this place in life. Do you have a platform you can use for furthering God's kingdom? Do you have authority that enables you to make decisions that honor Him? Perhaps you can look to your left and your right and see others who need to know the Savior.

You are where you are "for just such a time as this." Be a modern-day Esther. Take a risk as she did when she went before the king. There is great reward in knowing you are in the center of God's will.

Pray:

Lord, help me to be like Esther as I take risks for Your kingdom. Help me to trust You as she did when she went before the king, knowing that he could choose to end her life. I want to do Your will in my life regardless of the risk. I long to be a part of Your plans. Amen.

NEW HEAVEN AND NEW EARTH

Read REVELATION 21

Key Verses:

> "Look, God's home is now among his people! He will live with them, and they will be his people. God himself will be with them. He will wipe every tear from their eyes, and there will be no more death or sorrow or crying or pain. All these things are gone forever." And the one sitting on the throne said, "Look, I am making everything new!"
>
> REVELATION 21:3–5 NLT

Understand:

* Why do you think God didn't give us more detail about what life will be like in the new heaven and earth?

* Do you think the details we're given in Revelation are more literal or symbolic? Why?

Apply:

The Bible gives us some description and detail but doesn't tell us a whole lot about what forever life in the new heaven and earth will be like, probably because our minds couldn't fully understand how awesome it will be. First Corinthians

2:9 (NLT) says, "No eye has seen, no ear has heard, and no mind has imagined what God has prepared for those who love him." But God's Word does tell us everything will be new and spectacular in its architecture and beauty. Even better, there will be no more death or sorrow or crying or pain. Our dear heavenly Father will wipe every tear from our eyes Himself. We will have total peace and joy forever, with God making His home among us. Incredible! A lovely way to end your day is to praise and thank God for the perfect paradise He is creating for you and to fall asleep dreaming of what it might be like.

Pray:

Heavenly Father, I know the new heaven and earth will be incredible. It's beyond anything I can imagine, but it's still so fun to dream about. I thank You and praise You for the perfect forever You are preparing for all who love You and trust Jesus as Savior. Amen.

GOD'S DOING BIG THINGS

Read ISAIAH 43:14–21

Key Verse:

> *"For I am about to do something new. See, I have already begun! Do you not see it? I will make a pathway through the wilderness. I will create rivers in the dry wasteland."*
> ISAIAH 43:19 NLT

Understand:

* Recall a time when you know God moved in a mighty way to make something happen. How does it make you feel to know that He is ready to do something even greater?

* What is God doing in your life today?

* What's the biggest change for the better you can imagine in your life?

Apply:

We all have seasons of stagnation. There are times when we're unsatisfied with the way things are, but we are either unable or unwilling to make the adjustments necessary to change the situation. Maybe you're under an avalanche of debt. Maybe you have a relationship that is strained or breaking. Maybe you need to lose weight for the sake of your own health and your family, but the number on the scale hasn't budged in years.

Whatever situation you're thinking of, God is moving! Just like He did for the Israelites fleeing Egypt, He will make a way across the Red Sea when there seems to be no way. Here's the key: in order to get there, we must be following Him.

Are you willing to take the steps to allow God to change your situation? It may mean seeking help from experts; it may mean your time and resources. It will not be easy; it may not be quick—but God is faithful, and He is doing something new. Can you feel it?

Pray:

> *I'm ready for change, God. Lead me through this
> wilderness to Your promised land. Show me
> what You will have me do. Amen.*

PARTING THE SEA

Read EXODUS 14

Key Verse:

> Then Moses put out his hand over the sea.
> And the Lord moved the sea all night by a
> strong east wind. So the waters were divided.
> EXODUS 14:21 NLV

Understand:

* God moved in a mighty way to protect His children when He parted the Red Sea. What miracles has He performed on your behalf?

* When was the last time you faced a situation that seemed impassable, like Israel and the Red Sea? How did you make it through?

Apply:

Talk about an epic scene! This is one for the history books, filled with all the excitement and drama of a Hollywood movie. Picture the Israelites, on a trek out of Egypt across the desert. Enter Pharaoh's army, on the move to stop the Israelites in their tracks.

The Israelites come to the edge of the Red Sea. They're trapped, sick with worry and anxiety. There's no way across—no boats, no bridges, nothing. They're trapped, and the enemy is gaining ground. Surely all is about to be lost.

Then, in an astounding move, God pushes back the water. The Israelites pass through on dry land. Their enemy presses in hard behind them. . .and the waters rush over Pharaoh's army, killing them all.

This story of God's miraculous protection of His children should fill your heart with hope. If He was willing to change nature for the Hebrew children, what will He do for you?

Pray:

> *Lord, what a story! I wish I'd been there in person to
> witness the parting of the sea firsthand. Thank You
> for protecting Your children, both then and now. I'm so
> grateful Your protective hand is at work in my life. Amen.*

GOD'S FAITHFULNESS HAS NO END

Read DEUTERONOMY 7:6–9

Key Verse:

> *Know therefore that the LORD your God is God;*
> *he is the faithful God, keeping his covenant of*
> *love to a thousand generations of those who*
> *love him and keep his commandments.*
> DEUTERONOMY 7:9 NIV

Understand:

* How do you know you can trust God to keep His word?

* When has God been faithful to you despite your own unfaithfulness?

Apply:

We humans are a fickle bunch. We go from one fad diet to the next. Today's stunning interior design is tomorrow's cheesy, dated look. From today's bestselling author to tomorrow's newest big celebrity, our attention spans grow shorter by the minute.

Thank goodness our steady God doesn't follow whims or popular thought. When we have exhausted ourselves by trying to keep up with current trends and schools of thought, the Lord is steadfast in all things, not the least of which is that He will faithfully keep His promises to His children.

Maybe what you really need today is mental rest from chasing after the newest thing. Your loving Father provides that in His faithfulness. You don't need to wonder what He's thinking or what He's doing. He will not suddenly change His expectations or stop caring about you and move on to someone else. You have His love, and you have it forever.

Pray:

Father God, I praise You because of Your faithfulness. You are my rock and my strong fortress that cannot be moved. I don't have to fretfully wonder what You're doing in my life, because I trust You fully. Infuse my spirit with steadfastness in my relationships. I want to shine Your light of faithfulness to others in everyday life. Amen.

GOD HEARS AND LISTENS

Read PSALM 66

Key Verses:

> But truly God has listened; he has attended to the voice
> of my prayer. Blessed be God, because he has not rejected
> my prayer or removed his steadfast love from me!
>
> PSALM 66:19–20 ESV

Understand:

* What is the difference between hearing and listening?

* Scripture tells us that God both hears and listens to our
  prayers. Why are both important?

Apply:

Moms of young children are expert listeners. A child may talk
a mile a minute about a thousand things that seem to have
no common thread, but a mommy understands the precious
heart behind the words. She can truly listen to the little voice.

God accepts the prayers of His children in an even more
intimate way. He hears our voice. He listens and understands
our feelings and motivations behind the words. And because
He created us, He knows our true heart for the prayers we

pray. As imperfect and inarticulate as we often are when speaking to our Father, He welcomes our prayers and showers us in His love.

God is speaking into our lives as well. Do we hear? We must quiet the other voices and noisemakers in our lives and really listen. After speaking to God, sit in silence and ask Him to speak. The Holy Spirit will help you hear, listen, and understand the Father's voice. When you and God are both attending to each other's voice, there's no prayer more powerful!

Pray:

Father, thank You for hearing and listening to my voice when I call to You in prayer. When You listen, I feel loved, accepted, and understood. Today I am listening for You. Speak, Lord, and I will hear and understand. Amen.

A VICTORY HYMN

Read JUDGES 4–5

Key Verses:

Now Deborah, a prophetess, the wife of Lappidoth, was judging
Israel at that time. She used to sit under the palm of Deborah
between Ramah and Bethel in the hill country of Ephraim,
and the people of Israel came up to her for judgment.

JUDGES 4:4–5 ESV

Understand:

* This is one of the few times that a female is listed as
  a prophetess of God. What do you think of God using
  women in a role such as this?

* Why do you suppose Judges 5 recounts the same story
  as Judges 4, only in poetic form?

Apply:

Deborah was a prophetess of God and the only female judge
ever mentioned in the Bible. (Talk about being a standout!)
She sat under a palm tree between Ramah and Bethel in the
hill country, where people would come to her for judgment.

Deborah had a strong prophetic gifting. She shared with

Barak (a military commander of that time) that God had commanded him to attack Jabin, the king of Canaan, as well as Sisera, Jabin's military commander.

Stop and picture this for a moment. A woman, telling a man to attack and kill another man? In biblical times, this was almost unheard of.

Many would say that it should still be unheard of, that women are to be seen and not heard in church. There are a couple of scriptures that seem to lean in that direction. Taken in context (the culture of that day being quite different from today), some would argue that women have a perfect right to minister. Regardless of what you believe on that score, Deborah certainly led the way for godly women.

Pray:

> *Thank You for the reminder that women*
> *are usable, Lord! You've never excluded women*
> *from Your plan, and I'm so grateful. Amen.*

GOD SINGS OVER YOU

Read ZEPHANIAH 3

Key Verse:

"The LORD your God is with you; the mighty One will save you. He will rejoice over you. You will rest in his love; he will sing and be joyful about you."
ZEPHANIAH 3:17 NCV

Understand:

* What are the promises found in Zephaniah 3:17? Name each one.

* Which one are you in the deepest need of today?

Apply:

While this promise was originally for the Israelites, we know that these promises ring true for us today as well. God has saved you if you have put your faith in Christ (see Acts 4:12). You can rest in His unconditional love (see Matthew 11:28–30).

Does it bring you comfort today to know that as you rest in the Lord, He sings over you and takes great delight in you? Have you ever rocked one of your children to sleep, singing until those little eyelids just cannot remain open? There is nothing more peaceful and delightful than watching your child rest. This is how God feels about you!

Rest in the Lord. Take refuge from the busyness and difficulty of the world. Find peace in His arms, and allow your heavenly Father to sing over you until things seem a bit more manageable.

Pray:

Lord, hearing that You sing over me makes You seem very close rather than far away. I know that You desire for me to find my rest in You. Help me to trust You enough to relinquish even my deepest fears and sorrows to Your more than capable hands. In Jesus' name I pray. Amen.

GOD SEES

Read PROVERBS 15

Key Verse:

> *The eyes of the Lord are in every place,*
> *watching the bad and the good.*
> PROVERBS 15:3 NLV

Understand:

* There is so much pithy, practical wisdom to apply in Proverbs. What verses in chapter 15 have great impact on you tonight?

* When you're tempted to give a harsh word but instead hold your tongue and give a soft answer, what happens? Do you practice this discipline regularly?

Apply:

No one has vision like God does. The Bible says He sees and knows absolutely everything in every place. "No one can hide from God. His eyes see everything we do. We must give an answer to God for what we have done," says Hebrews 4:13 (NLV). And Job 28:24 (NLV) says, "He looks to the ends of the earth, and sees everything under the heavens." For people making bad choices and living lives of careless sin, those verses might be scary. But for those who love and want to follow and obey God's Word, they are wonderful and encouraging. God wants us to obey His good ways because He loves us and wants what's best for us. Trust that He always sees you in every moment of your life, and let that give you peace and courage that He's able to strengthen and encourage you at any time and in any situation.

Pray:

Heavenly Father, please remind me that You are always watching me in every place, in every moment, in every situation. Please let that truth encourage me and give me peace! Amen.

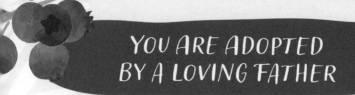

YOU ARE ADOPTED BY A LOVING FATHER

Read EPHESIANS 1:3–14

Key Verse:

> *God decided in advance to adopt us into his own family
> by bringing us to himself through Jesus Christ. This is
> what he wanted to do, and it gave him great pleasure.*
> EPHESIANS 1:5 NLT

Understand:

* How does knowing that God adopted His children into
  His family change your perception of your brothers and
  sisters in Christ?

* Jesus is God's only Son, but you are an adopted sister to
  Christ, with full privileges to share in the inheritance of
  God's kingdom. What does this mean to you?

Apply:

Adopting a child is a big undertaking. It's not just the time
and process—often filled with paperwork and protocol and
interviews and red tape; it's also a pricey endeavor, costing
anywhere from a few thousand dollars to much, much more.

But for parents who have already taken a child into their

heart and family, no paperwork is too lengthy. No red tape is too frustrating. No cost is too high. The child is already perfectly loved, well before signatures are on the adoption papers.

So much more is our heavenly Father's love for you. God set the adoption into motion, and your Savior and Brother, Jesus, cut through the red tape and paid the ultimate price to make sure you could become His sister.

Today, thank God for making your adoption and salvation a family affair, dear one. God's grace and kindness cover you, His daughter.

Pray:

> Father, I am overwhelmed when I consider the fact
> that You see me as worthy of being Your adopted,
> chosen daughter. Because of my Brother, Jesus,
> You see me as holy and blameless. I don't deserve
> such favor, but I gratefully accept it. Amen.

GUARD YOUR TONGUE

Read JAMES 3:1–12

Key Verse:

*For if we could control our tongues, we would be perfect
and could also control ourselves in every other way.*
JAMES 3:2 NLT

Understand:

* In what situations are you most likely to lose control of
  your tongue?

* James likens the tongue to a flame of fire (James 3:6).
  When have you seen words create devastation like an
  out-of-control fire?

* When have you held your tongue despite wanting to say
  something? How did it make you feel?

Apply:

If you're doing this study early in the morning, maybe you
haven't had a chance to open mouth, insert foot yet—the
day is still young. James 3:8 tells us that unlike all kinds of
animals, birds, reptiles, and fish that can be trained and
tamed, no one can tame the tongue.

So, if we can't tame it, we must keep it under lock and key. Proverbs 21:23 (ESV) tells us, "Whoever keeps his mouth and his tongue keeps himself out of trouble." Psalm 34:13 (NLT) says to "keep your tongue from speaking evil and your lips from telling lies!" God has given us speech for a reason, and from our words can come encouraging, life-giving hope. But we must learn to listen first, consider second, and answer (when necessary) third. Ask God for the words He would have you say (or not say), and He will help you use your words wisely.

Pray:

Father, only You can help me get a handle on this powerful muscle in my mouth. My tongue gets me into trouble too often, but I also admit that I too often react with my tongue. Give me the wisdom to know when and what to speak and when to remain silent. Amen.

THE RIGHT PEOPLE, PLACES, AND DETAILS

Read JOSHUA 2

Key Verses:

> The king of Jericho sent to Rahab, saying, "Bring out the
> men who have come to you, who entered your house,
> for they have come to search out all the land." But the
> woman had taken the two men and hidden them.
> JOSHUA 2:3–4 ESV

Understand:

* Have you experienced a time when you could clearly
  see God's hand through the people He made available to
  you exactly when you needed them?

* What tiny details have you seen God's hand in as He
  helps and directs you?

Apply:

The two men Joshua sent to spy on the land of Canaan had
to be anxious about their mission. Hopefully, you're not
facing anything quite so dangerous as they did; but whatever
stressful thing might be weighing heavily on you today, let
the story be an encouragement to you. God provides the right
people in the right places to help you in your troubles, just like

He provided Rahab to help hide and protect the two spies in her home. She told them that she trusted in their God. In turn, the spies promised to help protect Rahab and her family as long as she did not tell anyone about their plans. Then Rahab lowered them by a rope through the window and urged them to hide for three days in the hill country before returning home. Later, with that same red rope, the spies knew where to find her and her family to protect them from being killed when the Israelites took over Jericho.

Pray:

> *Heavenly Father, thank You for the way You orchestrate exactly the right people in exactly the right places with exactly the right details to help those who love and follow You. I trust that You do that for me, and I'm so grateful. Amen.*

THIS BIBLE WILL HELP YOU STUDY GOD'S WORD!

Holy Bible KJV: 5-Minute Bible Study Edition

Barbour's 5-Minute Bible Study series has sold hundreds of thousands of copies. . . . Now, that powerful content has been combined with the beloved King James Version of the Bible.

Here are the complete Old and New Testaments, along with 26 sections of 5-Minute Bible Study content, featuring

- ✳ a key scripture for consideration
- ✳ questions to encourage deeper thought
- ✳ a devotional application
- ✳ a thoughtful prayer starter
- ✳ ample writing space

This Bible is a powerful tool for your spiritual growth. . .and makes an excellent keepsake of your journey.

Hardback / 978-1-63609-799-2